In God Met Me Here, *through vulnerable* [...] *real life stories…stories that will inspire you, challenge you, and remind you that God doesn't desire "Super-Christians," but instead desires an authentic relationship with His children. A relationship that is formed out of dependence on Him and trusting in Him. You will be blessed by* God Met Me Here*!*

Eric Ferguson
Author. Entrepreneur. Pastor.

This book illuminates the truth that God will never leave us, even during our toughest times. Each story was selected to help both the author and the reader increase their faith. These untold stories needed to be told for such a time as this, for His glory.

Pastor Monica L. Gilbert
Senior Pastor, Rivers of Living Waters Fellowship

Satan and his spirits "prowls through the world seeking the ruin of souls." The poison of drugs is one of the devil's most damning. That evil was presented in Felisa's life, but she chose to cast it down to the abyss of hell. Her faith was challenged but she never wavered because the Lord met her and His love for her guided her to His arms. She is a woman of true faith in her never-ending love for God.

Randy Saucedo
Founder, S.A.V.E (Survivors Against Violence Everywhere)

God is a God of miracles and many chances!!! His love and mercy are endless as demonstrated by each person's story in which life was broken and transformed into one of wholeness and restoration!!!

Diane Ham
Follower and lover of Jesus Christ

Kingdom Publishing Presents

God Met Me Here

Trust the Tug.

In love,

Kingdom Publishing Presents

God Met Me Here

Stories of how God shows up in everyday life.

KINGDOM
PUBLISHING

We would like to acknowledge the following individuals for permission to print the following material.

Shattered Pipe Dream. Reprinted by permission of Felisa B. Jack © 2019 Felisa B. Jack.

God is Calling the Shots. Reprinted by permission of Scottie Dyess © 2019 Scottie Dyess.

Hostage Situation. Reprinted by permission of Maggie Ingram © 2019 Maggie Ingram.

I Just Wanna Be Happy. Reprinted by permission of Sharese Hudley © 2019 Sharese Hudley.

Trust the Tug. Reprinted by permission of Lori Ashworth © 2019 Lori Ashworth.

100% Dad. Reprinted by permission of Nik Ingram © 2019 Nik Ingram.

In Good Times and in Bad. Reprinted by permission of Beatrice Bruno © 2019 Beatrice Bruno.

It's Never Too Late. Reprinted by permission of Donna Schooler © 2019 Donna Schooler.

The Dream. Reprinted by permission of Nik & Maggie Ingram © 2019 Nik & Maggie Ingram.

Line In the Sand. Reprinted by permission of Tracy Fagan © 2019 Tracy Fagan.

Temporal Sight. Reprinted by permission of Teresa Blaes © 2019 Teresa Blaes.

A Place Where I Became Desperate. Reprinted by permission of Dr. Jimmie Reed © 2019 Dr. Jimmie Reed.

A Swim with the Angels. Reprinted by permission of Linda R. Robin © 2019 Linda R. Robin.

Cover Design: Tracy Fagan

ISBN 978-1-7333078-1-9 (print)

ISBN 978-1-7333078-2-6 (ebook)

Table of Contents

*Some names and identifying details have been changed to protect the privacy of individuals.

Introduction

I am so glad this book found its way into your hands. It is no coincidence you are reading this sentence right now. The truth is, the One who created you, God, LOVES YOU DEARLY! He has since before you were ever born. He will continue to love you forever - no matter what! And, God loves to hear from you... yes, you. He is calling you into relationship with Him, and I believe He is meeting you right here, right now.

In the pages of this book, there is an experience that was lived out and the story told to touch your heart. In other words, God has moved mountains to meet you right here through the pages of this book!

If you have never had a relationship with God, or if you had one that has faded, I would ask that you keep an open mind as you read the stories in this book. Instead of saying, "There is no way that can be true!!!" come with the mindset, "If that really is true, God, please show me!" If you have just an ever-so-tiny amount of faith that God just might be real, and you ask Him to reveal Himself to you, I believe He will.

As you dive into these amazing stories, keep in mind, some of these authors had a close relationship with God at the time when He met them. Some authors had walked away from their relationship with God, while others had never known God personally. I point this out to let you know that no matter which category you find yourself in, the Bible tells us in Romans 2:11 that God doesn't have partiality among us. He loves each and every one of us and wants to be in relationship with you.

God reminds us several times in His Word that He will never leave us nor forsake us. In other words, He is ALWAYS with us. However, in each of our lives, we can look back and find specific times when He met us right there! It is those times when you sit there in amazement with what just happened...or didn't happen. And there is no other explanation except God.

God gave me the inspiration to write this book through an experience where He met me...at the intersection of Potomac St. and Broncos Parkway in Centennial, Colorado.

> *My daughter and I were leaving Bible study. That night the discussion was about being in God's grace versus His mercy. My daughter was driving home, and we were about ½ mile from the church. She was getting ready to turn left - and she had the green arrow. As she started to go, God brought to my attention a car that was driving towards the intersection at full speed. I then saw a brief vision of a horrific accident. Out of my mouth came the stern command, "STOP!" My daughter reacted immediately. The black SUV came barreling through his red light and didn't hit his brakes until after he was all the way through the intersection. Immediately, I knew that God had saved our lives. When thanking God for what He had done, I heard Him say, "Tracy, I met you here; right at the corner of Potomac St. and Broncos Parkway."*

When God meets people, it isn't always through a drastic, life-saving situation. Sometimes it is through simple small signs or nudges. For example, I have a dear friend that, when she is feeling alone and like she can't hear God, she will ask for a sign that He is near. He will send a car with a personalized license plate to intercept her path and remind her of His love for her. Some examples of the plates include, "GODANDI," "IAMHIS."

In the stories that follow, you will begin to gain an understanding of who God is and how He protects and leads us through different situations and circumstances. Notice He doesn't always take the situations or circumstances away, but will meet you right where you are to help you navigate through the trial. Even in His Word He promises us that we will experience trouble in this world. Jesus promises us His peace because He has overcome the world. (John 16:33)

As you read the stories in this book, keep in mind God placed this book in your hands because He wants a personal relationship with you. To learn more about what this means and how to begin this relationship, go to page 89. There, I will share with you more about what it means to be saved and share a prayer with you that will ask Jesus into your heart.

For now, I invite you to jump in and be encouraged as you read these stories of our amazing God and His love for His children.

Shattered Pipe Dream
Felisa B. Jack

I awoke to a mess: overflowing ashtrays, empty beer cans, and liquor bottles, as well as numerous cigarette lighters piled on the table like a deck of cards. To say that I 'awoke' is not as relevant as the fact that I had actually gone to sleep after being awake for 2 straight days and nights smoking crack.

It all began one evening, 3 months prior, when a long-time friend, Aaron, and his Uncle Ron came by for a visit. Happy to see my old friend and meet his favorite uncle, I welcomed them in. Per usual, Aaron arrived with a 12-pack of beer and a bottle of brandy. We spent time catching up. I got to know his uncle whose easy manner and quirky sense of humor quickly made him 'family' to me, too.

While imbibing in our adult libations, Aaron began to share with me that his Uncle Ron had a heroin habit and how he had a plan to get him off the needle.

"Okaaay, how do you plan to do that and what does that have to do with me?" I thought warily.

Before I could verbalize the question, Aaron quickly began telling me how much he trusted me and that I was the only person he would do this with.

He went on to explain that he had discovered something that might replace the heroin; that was less lethal than possibly overdosing with a needle in his arm.

"Less LETHAL? That still doesn't sound good", I mused.

I'll admit though, I was a little intrigued as Aaron seemed very sure of himself. I was always that one who was willing to try (just about) anything at least once. Live on the edge. Take risks. Isn't that what made life exhilarating? Yeah, I was a little crazy back then.

"Whatcha got?" I asked.

In one fluid movement, he produced a little plastic bag and a glass pipe from his jacket pocket. It contained what looked to me like 3 medium-sized aquarium rocks.

Confused, I asked, "What is THAT supposed to be?"

"It's just some rock, sis", he replied.

"Well yeah, that's what they look like, but what IS it?" I repeated.

"Rock cocaine", he laughingly replied, as though he couldn't believe I was so uninformed.

Well, I was. I knew what cocaine was and had even snorted some before. But this, this was definitely not something you would put up your nose. He then plopped down at my kitchen table and pulled a lighter and a razor blade from another pocket. Still baffled, I watched as he sliced off a piece of the 'rock', put it in the bowl of the pipe, and put the lighter to it as he slowly inhaled. A pearly white mist began to flow through the neck of the pipe. He held the smoke in his lungs for several seconds and then exhaled.

"Hmmm... that looks easy enough", I contemplated.

He then passed it to me, instructing me on how to do what he had just done. So I put the pipe to my mouth and followed his instruction. The effect was immediate…and intense. I'd never experienced anything like it. That first hit was like a catapult to the moon. Everything I knew, felt, and thought dissipated much like the smoke. Instant euphoria. Little did I know how much I would want to recapture that feeling.

Next it was Uncle Ron's turn. Skeptical but willing to attain any high he could get, he did as we had done. He was equally enthralled by the feeling of being transported to another place, free from his cares. Aaron looked at me, I looked at him, and we both looked at Uncle Ron. Our looks spoke our thoughts.

"Maybe this WILL get him off the needle." It was evident that he was really enjoying the high. "Hmmm", I thought. "He can get off the needle and just smoke a pipe. Clearly, it was the lesser of two evils, right?"

Don't get it twisted. Proverbs 16:25 tells us, *"There is a way that seems right to a man, but its end is the way of death."* (NKJV)

The high was intense, but short-lived (about 15 minutes). We ran through those few 'rocks' in no time. Our bodies immediately craved more, but that wasn't an option. Aaron pulled the beer from the refrigerator and broke the seal on the brandy. He knew that alcohol would be the only thing to take the edge off and get that monkey off our backs. It worked, and we spent the balance of the night talking, playing dominoes, and getting drunk. After they left, I went to bed. Well, passed out is more accurate.

The next day I recalled that incredible feeling I'd gotten from smoking crack, but foolishly just chalked it up to yet another thing I had experimented with. No harm. No foul. But still....I had really liked it. I'd heard the stories of those that had become addicted; selling their belongings, stealing, and even performing sexual acts, just for a hit.

"Now that's just crazy, pathetic, and irresponsible", I scoffed. "I work hard, pay my bills and take care of my child. I would never let anything have that kind of control over me." I was so sure of myself, in control (or so I thought,) and prideful; but Proverbs 16:18 says, *"Pride goes before destruction. And a haughty spirit before a fall."* (NKJV)

And fall, I did. I'd let the enemy trick me into thinking that I was in total control; I just needed to be smart when I indulged. If I was going to smoke, I had to make sure that I had 3 things: dope, alcohol and cigarettes. I mean, that's what worked the first time, right? I had it all figured out. Easy-peasy. However, 1 Peter 5:8 warns us to, *"Be sober, be vigilant, because your adversary, the devil, walks about like a roaring lion seeking whom he may devour."* (NKJV)

My 'smart plan' was no match for the schemes of the enemy. He was after my life, and my living in rebellion against God left me wide open for him to come in and carry out his mission: *"...to kill, steal and destroy."* (John 10:10, NKJV)

My life took a rapid downward spiral as one day, desperate to get high, I quit my job. Brilliant, right? Well, my thought process was, if I quit, they would have to give me my final check that day. Wrong. They politely informed me that I would get paid on my regularly scheduled payday.

"What?!? I should've gotten myself fired; then, they would've had to pay me that day," I lamented. Now what was I going to do? I needed a plan, a plot, a hustle. Something to get money for the drug my body was screaming for. Oh, but the enemy knew my state of mind, and the very next evening he played his trump card.

Once again, Aaron and Uncle Ron were at my door with the same combo as before: beer, liquor, and crack. But THIS time, Uncle Ron wanted to make sure we 'had enough' to smoke longer than last time. He wanted to 'Go big tonight.' With a pocketful of cash, he began to ask about prices and quantities. He asked Aaron what we'd had last time. Aaron told him it was a half a gram.

"Well, what's the next size up?" Uncle Ron asked. Aaron began to run it down to him: a half was $50, a gram $100, and an 8-ball $300.

Uncle Ron didn't hesitate. "How much do we get with an 8-ball?"

"It's about 3- $100 rocks", Aaron replied.

"Let's do it! We can each have our own. Call your connect!" Uncle Ron exclaimed. Aaron and I were literally dumbfounded. What we didn't know was that a heroin high and a crack high are very different in duration. Uncle Ron, because he was used to heroin, needed more than the average person to attain the high he was used to. It looked like it was going to be a long night.

But...the concept of having my own to myself was exciting and a little scary at the same time. Do you know how long it takes to smoke a gram by yourself? About 2 full days! We smoked night and day, with a little drinking in between, until FINALLY it was gone and we drank until we passed out. As I said at the beginning of my story, as I perused my living room once I came to, I was mortified. I began to see that I was taking one drug to counteract another drug, compounded by excessive cigarette smoking. I felt like garbage. Suddenly it all seemed so pointless and I had such emptiness inside.

I remember hearing Bishop T.D. Jakes once saying, "If you think your finite will is any match for God's infinite Will, you are trippin'!" I know that God gives us free will, but I believe there are times when the path we are on is going to take us so far away from His plans and purposes for our lives, He will supernaturally intervene and take control of the mess we've made.

In that moment, God opened my eyes, overshadowed me with His love, and delivered me instantly from crack...**Instantly.** Sounds impossible, right?

Well, *"with God ALL things are possible."* (Matthew 19:26, NKJV) I opened my sliding glass door and threw out every glass pipe, every glass vial, and every lighter. The glass shattering on the pavement below startled my houseguests awake. They thought I had gone crazy. I told them that I'd never felt better and they needed to leave. Completely bewildered, (and a little scared,) they beat a hasty retreat.

I felt free for the first time in months. I knew something had happened deep inside me, in my heart and in my mind. I knew OF God, but didn't have a relationship with Him. But He wanted one...**with** me. I love what the Bible says in Romans 5:8, *"But God demonstrates His own love toward us, in that while we were still sinners, Christ died for us."* (NKJV)

I could have died the first time I smoked crack. I had many friends who did. But God met me in a crack pipe and His love delivered me...**Completely.** I owe Him my life and it is my joy to honor Him with it every day.

Felisa B. Jack

 Felisa B. Jack is passionate about God and sharing His unadulterated Word to uplift and encourage others and to see souls saved. Her outreach ministry, *Precious 2 Him Ministries*, was born from her deep desire to remind people that they are indeed valuable and precious to God. Felisa believes we overcome by the word of our testimony, and openly shares how the power of God delivered her from domestic violence, divorce, and substance abuse.

She is an author, minister and speaker. She shares her testimony of how God pulled her out of a life threatening domestic violence relationship in her book, *Pursued: A Testimony of God's Relentless Love*. Please contact her directly for interviews or speaking requests.

 www.precs2him.com

@PRECS2HM

God is Calling the Shots

Scottie Dyess

I have struggled with depression and anxiety since I was a little boy. My parents divorced when I was just a baby. I lived with my mother most of the time and only saw my dad on holidays. Going to my dad's house was never easy because my stepmom at the time was very abusive; physically and verbally. My stepmom and my dad would continuously tell me how worthless I was. When I returned home, my mother would ensure me that I was not worthless, and I could do anything I set my mind to do.

Having two opposing voices speaking in my life as a child really messed me up inside. It was so confusing.

In school, I was bullied for being too skinny, not fitting in, being poor, etc. As I got older, it seemed like every relationship I ever got in, whether it was friends, family, girlfriends, etc., always seemed to fall apart — and I saw myself as the common denominator.

Although I grew up in church, I always thought Jesus and the stories in the Bible were nothing more than fairytales. I thought, "How can Jesus be real if all of this bad stuff has happened to me?" In September of 2011, I began to learn just how real this Jesus is.

My dad was going through a divorce with my stepmom when something changed in him. He began attending church and got baptized. I did not really understand it, but when I saw this stone-hearted man change, I knew this Jesus had to be real. My dad gave me this little black booklet with a prayer on the back. I thought about that prayer a lot. I remember walking outside and sitting on my dad's front porch, getting down on my knees, and saying that little prayer. As the words came out of my mouth, I saw a star shooting across the sky.

When I got back home to Louisiana, I cut off the relationship with my dad because I felt he had to focus on his stuff, and I felt the need to focus on Jesus. I gave my life to Christ and got baptized. From there, I studied the Word and learned a lot about Jesus. I would go outside and fellowship with the Lord and stars would shoot in the sky.

In 2013, my relationship with the Lord grew much deeper. In January, I received the infilling of the Holy Spirit. Shortly after, I experienced the passing of my grandfather, Bruce Cunningham. Losing him changed me. It was the first time I had ever experienced the death of someone close to me. My grandfather had protected my mother and me when we moved to Louisiana.

In March of that year, following my grandfather's death, I was anointed to be a prophet with the spirit of Elisha. Continuing on this journey, I kept learning and fellowshipping with the Lord. During this time, I had many girlfriends and relationships along the way that always fell apart.

After high school, I didn't have any plans to go to college, mainly because I didn't know what I wanted to be when I grew up. That summer, thoughts of suicide troubled my mind and landed me in a mental health institution. Shortly after I got out of the mental institution, I felt the Lord lead me to Actors, Models, and Talents for Christ (AMTC). That same year, I met Tina. As we grew in our relationship and because I didn't want to experience another failed relationship, we decided to have sex outside of marriage, hoping that would keep us together. In reality, the only thing it did was steer me away from the Lord.

In the summer of 2015, after a couple of months of training with AMTC in Dallas, Texas, I went with the organization to Orlando, Florida to do a show. Tina came with me. After finishing the show, I received a ton of callbacks. I continued to pursue AMTC and the callbacks I received after leaving Orlando; nothing really came of any of it.

Tina and I decided to get married. Shortly after our wedding, I became extremely sick. I had a gallbladder attack that caused me to lose a lot of weight, landing me in the hospital in February 2016. Not only was I dealing with health issues, I also experienced another instance of feeling worthless when my wife chose to go partying with her friends in another city versus standing by my side.

Our relationship continued to take the course of a roller-coaster…up and down and up and down. It included fights, break-ups, make-ups, and even a night in jail for me. I became so angry with the Lord; I walked away from the church completely for two years. I cursed His name, screamed at Him at night, and just let out so much hatred towards Him.

I was so angry at God! One time, I walked out into the pouring rain while it was lightning and thundering, taunting Him to strike me down. That night, after stumbling in drunk from the bar, He responded to my rant by giving me a dream. In the dream, I was drinking and partying. Suddenly, the music stopped. I walked over to the bartender and asked what was going on; I wanted to know why the music stopped. The bartender walked away from me; the crowd followed behind her.

Then, this one lady walked up to me and called me by name. "Scottie, what are you doing here?"

I said, "I'm drinking and having a good time."

She responded, "No, Scottie. You don't belong here. You need to get back in church." I woke up. I was filled with anger.

I remember telling God to just leave me alone. I stopped going to the bars and instead thought I would outsmart God and sneak alcohol in my grandmother's house. Despite all of my rebellion, I never got caught by my grandmother, and I was still being blessed with promotions on my job.

During the summer of 2016, I quickly began another relationship with Jena. It lasted a little over a year and then fell apart. It seemed like door after door after door in my life kept closing. The acting, the relationships, even trying to buy my own house — nothing in my life seemed to ever go right. I blasphemed God. I cursed at Him. I was tired of hurting people because of my depression. I was tired of my depression deepening with every disappointment. I was tired of this weight on my shoulders. I came to the conclusion: the best solution would be to end it all.

December 13, 2017 is a day I will never forget. After a long, hard day at work, I finally returned home at 9:00 PM. I was exhausted from the day and tired of life. The depression and anxiety had been getting worse ever since I walked away from the church. At the end of my rope, I grabbed the Taurus 9mm from underneath my bed, stuck it in my jacket pocket, and headed out my bedroom door.

My grandmother came out of the bathroom door at the same moment and asked me if everything was okay. I lied and told her I was fine; I just needed some fresh air. When I opened the door, a star shot across the sky. My eyes quickly filled with tears. I rushed out the door.

I got in my car and balled my eyes out. I knew it was The Lord who shot the star across the night sky just like He did when I was a teen.

As I drove off, my stepdad called. He suggested I take my mom Christmas shopping. His thoughts were on caring for my mom for the upcoming holiday season; here I was with a gun in my pocket, about to commit suicide. I told him I loved him and I could not do this anymore and hung up the phone. He called back. I told him the same thing. After he realized what I meant, I heard his keys rattling in the background as he ran for his truck. I hung up the phone.

My grandmother called and I told her the same thing.

Then…my mom called: my rock, the woman who carried me in her womb for nine months. The hardest part was telling her I loved her and that I did not want to be here anymore.

I reached the end of LA 846 and stepped out of my car. I put the gun to my head and looked up to the night sky.

I said, *"God I don't want to be here anymore. I want to die, but I don't want to go to hell."*

A star shot through the sky. I pulled the trigger…the bullet ejected itself. Instead of going through the barrel, the whole bullet came out of the top of the weapon. I reloaded the gun and tried again.

This time, angrily with tears in my eyes, I said, *"God I Don't Want To Be Here Anymore. I Want To Die But I Don't Want To Go To Hell!!"*

I pulled the trigger. It was as if time froze for five seconds. I watched that bullet go up, come right in front of my face…and land at my feet.

I was so embarrassed! I had told my family I was going to commit suicide and the gun didn't fire. I ran away. I got in my car and drove for two and a half hours into Arkansas. I pulled into a church parking lot and slept in my car that night.

December 15th, I paid cash for one night at a hotel in Arkansas.

December 16th, I came back to Louisiana and slept in my car.

I waited until December 17th, Sunday morning, for my grandmother to leave for church. After she left, I quickly gathered some clothes and took a shower. When I finished, I grabbed the gun and walked outside. This time, I pointed the gun at a box and pulled the trigger. The gun fired! I dropped the gun. I did not know what to say or think. I quickly got my clothes and the gun and left.

I started driving south and crossed over into Mississippi. Trying to go and get something to eat, I took a wrong turn. I didn't really know where I was headed…I just kept driving.

I finally reached Columbia, Mississippi. By the time I got there, the fog became so dense; I could not see the red tail lights of the car in front of me. It just so happened, though, that I was right by my dad's house. I felt I had no other choice than to stop at his place.

After I told him what had happened with me, he suggested we go for a drive. Protesting, I told him, "The fog is so thick, you can't see anything."

Acknowledging the fog, he assured me, "Don't worry. We'll be all right." As we started driving, the fog miraculously cleared up.

After staying at my dad's for two weeks, I began to think about leaving, no specific destination in mind. My dad and I went to grab a bite to eat. As we passed Woodlawn Church, the sign out front read, "You Belong Here." Those words pierced my heart.

Wednesday, January 3, 2018 was the first time I attended Woodlawn Church.

I received a refilling of the Holy Spirit on January 28, 2018.

On February 25, I was baptized in Jesus' name.

In March, I returned home to Louisiana and reconciled with my family. I officially moved to Columbia to attend Purpose Institute and fellowship at Woodlawn Church. God set me back on track to pursue my call to be a prophet of Jesus Christ with the spirit of Elisha anointing.

I blasphemed God. I cursed at Him. I rebelled against Him. In the end, God still met me and saved me from complete destruction. No matter who you are, what you have done, or where you have been, cry out to Jesus Christ - He can meet you and save you, too.

Scottie Dyess

Scottie Dyess is a powerful Man of God. He has experienced the trials of rejection and abuse. After a profound experience with God through a failed suicide attempt he became clear on his purpose and calling in life. Currently a student at Purpose Institute, he is studying their Apostolic curriculum and is in the process of receiving his Associate's degree. Scottie is passionate about serving others, children's ministry, and spreading the gospel of Jesus Christ. His main goal is to one day evangelize around the world; healing the sick, bringing light to the uttermost parts of the earth, prophesying, and truly fulfilling his calling as a prophet with the spirit of Elisha.

@scottie.dyess

@scottie_dyess

Scottie Dyess

scottiedyess

Hostage Situation
Maggie Ingram

I was relieved when my parents got a divorce!

For years I had been aware that our lives were less than ideal. My dad had been an alcoholic since before I was born. He was mentally, physically, and verbally abusive to my mom. More times than I can count, my younger siblings, my mom, and I spent sleepless nights wondering where he was if he didn't come home or carefully avoiding him if he did. If he came home, he would usually start a fight with my mom that would end in him passing out; but not before an explosion of anger.

One night, when I was about five, he came home drunk. He ripped the handle from the door to their room, dragged my mom out and slung her around the house, pushed over a gun case, then brought her back to the room where he pushed her to the floor and tried to strangle her.

She then closed her eyes and started praying. Dad became so infuriated, he stood up and pulled back his foot to kick her in the head. I had been watching through the hole in the door where the handle had been and walked in right before he kicked.

Upon my entering the room, he kicked a bedside table instead and split the two inch thick solid oak side of the table. I'm confident that if he had kicked her head, it would have killed her. After a few days, he sobered up and apologized.

We went back to our normal like we had so many times before and we would so many times after that day.

That wasn't the first and it certainly wasn't the last time our lives were in danger. Finally after fourteen years of abuse and several affairs later, when I was eight years old, my mom left my dad.

Even at eight years old, I knew this was a turning point for my family. I was so happy to be away from my dad that I never really understood the impact divorce could have on a child. I was the oldest and too mature for my age. I was extra aware of everything and very grateful to be free even though that meant I would have to take on more responsibility. Sometimes, I overheard my mom in her room crying and praying out of desperation. When I look back, I realize that she really struggled to raise three children on her own, but I never felt any regret for having to help her out.

Added to the abuse from my father, we started going to a church that wasn't accepting of us. For the remainder of my childhood, the church and the church's school caused us to suffer more abuse and mistreatment. For years, we begged our mom to move back to Louisiana where her family lived, but we stayed. I will never forget when a little boy in our church passed away. The mother of that little boy, the principle of the school, came to my desk, got down in my face, and told me that it should have been my brother that died instead of her son. Her reasoning for this is because my mom was sinful and she'd never done anything wrong. I was crushed. We stood by that family while their son/brother fought for his life in the hospital for a little over a month. We prayed and begged God for a miracle. He was my brother's best friend and his sister was mine and my sister's best friend. Those words cut me deeper than anything ever had.

There were many more instances like this. The proverbial straw that broke the camel's back, though, was when I, out of desperation for someone to realize the deep pain I was in, ran away from home. I was gone to my grandmothers for about four days. When I returned, the principle had expelled me from the school and the pastor ostracized me from the youth group.

Finally, when I was nearly nineteen, I left home. I met my husband, we married, and five years later, had a daughter. In 2014, we had just finished renovating my dream home. We had a perfect two-year old little girl with tight red curls, big blue eyes, and a squeaky little voice. Life was perfect.

It was mid-July and I had spent the summer becoming increasingly more aware of a terrorist group that was wreaking havoc on the Middle East and making horrific threats to America. Before I knew it, I was not just following this group, I was obsessing over them and starting to find myself checking to see if they had made it to the United States yet. It wasn't long before I was losing sleep, staring out of windows, and avoiding going out into public.

To make matters worse, I spent all of my days clinging to my daughter and crying, begging God not to take her from me. I asked my husband to start disaster prepping and started making plans of what to do if we were ever attacked. I spent the next couple of months living in constant fear. I didn't sleep, I didn't eat, and I didn't enjoy life. I just prayed and cried, begging God not to take my family from me.

One night, the train that normally passed by our house twice a day stopped right outside our house. That had never happened before so I started to panic. I was frantically walking around the house, trying to convince Nik that a terrorist group had hijacked the train and was coming for us. At first, he didn't believe me. I persisted so he decided to humor me.

The train began making some loud "air release" noises and its lights were flashing. Then, two dark figures began moving around in the engine of the train. Nik walked out onto the porch and a "creepy white van" pulled up and proceeded to unload what looked like large duffle bags. Nik was finally concerned at this point. He paced back and forth on the front porch for about ten minutes with his AR-15! Lucky for us, one of our neighbors happened to work for the Sheriff's Department. Nik called the deputy to come investigate what was happening. The deputy arrived and Nik decided to join him on our golf cart, carrying his assault rifle.

The deputy shined his light and motioned for Nik to come over. Nik slowly walked down and out from behind the deputy. He saw one of his high school friends who was the engineer on the train! The engineer friend explained that they had to stop because they were over their hours and had to switch shifts. Nik and his friend had a good laugh about me thinking the terrorists had landed outside our house. I was later spotted by that train engineer and a friend overheard him say that I was the lady that was scared terrorists were invading her house.

That was really embarrassing. I knew I had to do something to change. That same friend finally suggested that I go see her therapist. I didn't want anyone to know I was actually going crazy, but I was desperate for help and the news was starting to get out; so I agreed.

Two weeks into therapy, I had a really good grasp on things. My amazing therapist listened to things I would say like, "This isn't like me. I've always been strong. No matter what has ever happened, I'm the one that stays calm and level headed." Then, I proceeded to list all the instances in which I was strong and the number of people who depended on me being strong.

I was strong and unaffected by my life and wore it like a badge of honor. My therapist helped me realized that, rather than being unaffected, I had merely been surviving. At the moment of my first childhood trauma, my mind kicked into survival mode. I spent the next twenty-plus years of my life surviving. Through all the loss I had suffered and the abuse and abandonment from my father, I had developed a distorted view of who God is and had come to not trust Him.

When I realized that, my entire life flashed before my eyes. I finally understood why I suddenly struggled with fear and anxiety and realized that this also tied into the severe social anxiety I'd been plagued with my entire life. I decided to continue my therapy. My therapist and I worked diligently for four months to strip away all the calluses, lies, distorted truths, pain, and mistrust to expose my heart to who God really is. God met me there.

In that room, in the corner of our church, every Tuesday morning at eleven, the God of the universe met me. He took the time to nurture my newfound faith in Him. I felt like a little girl riding her bike without training wheels for the first time, and God was my Father, holding on to the seat continually affirming...

"I'm still here!"

"I'm still holding you!"

"You're doing great!"

For the first time in my life, I was beginning to see God for who He is: a loving Father rather than an inaccessible deity towering over me waiting for the opportunity to force me to prove my love and devotion to Him through sacrifice. I spent four months diving into His love, drinking it in so emphatically I could barely breathe most of the time. Some days when I walked into therapy and my therapist asked how things had been for me since our last meeting, I'd just burst into tears. I would start with a series of "Did you know..." questions and insert all the things I'd learned about God that week and how He had been a very real and almost tangible presence in my life. My therapist would just smile and give me more scripture to read to learn more about my new Father.

At the beginning of my fifth month of therapy, my therapist released me and I graduated therapy! I had spent the days before my session with several groups of people that were here in our town helping us recover from a devastating tornado. On that morning of my therapy session, I had just left a meeting in which they named my husband the volunteer coordinator and me the lead case manager for the relief efforts. We would spend the next year leading the recovery efforts for Columbia Strong.

At that very moment, I reached the place God was leading me to. He revealed His purpose for me and He began using everything I'd been learning to heal a town of hurting people.

I Just Wanna Be Happy

Sharese Hudley

I recall hearing that Kirk Franklin song, "Wanna Be Happy?" and thinking to myself that nothing in my life was making me happy. I didn't know what I needed to do to be happy. I remember a time when I was happy but lonely. I met this guy at work named Scott. He was unlike anyone else I had dated. He was quiet; he kept to himself. For some reason, he was fascinating to me. We started talking. Not long after that, we became intimate. During this time, I was convicted about being saved and fornicating. I decided we would get married. The foundation for marriage wasn't there. It fell apart shortly thereafter. The only reason I wanted to get married was so I could please God and my man; I wouldn't be fornicating anymore. The marriage was so bad, we stopped having sex. We were always fighting and stopped spending time together. We didn't sleep in the same bed anymore; we didn't even sleep on the same floor.

During the marriage we had a child. It was a rough pregnancy and I was on bed rest most of the time. I had a complication during the delivery leaving me in pain most of the time. I couldn't get out of bed. I couldn't walk. I was unable to care for my newborn baby. Sitting up and holding her was very painful and I was always sick. Life became very difficult for me. I was oppressed and depressed. Most days I didn't get out of bed, or even out of the house.

Someone told me that if I smoked marijuana, it would take the nausea and pain away. So I did. It wasn't the first time, but it had been several years since the last time I smoked it. I had forgotten everything I learned in AA. I had attended AA shortly after I turned 21. I had started drinking and smoking in High School. Losing my virginity brought back memories of being molested. I used drugs and alcohol to try to drown out the pain. It was only a temporary fix. Once the high was gone, the memories and depression came back. I tried to take my life, but God kept me.

Before I was with Scott, I had already been going through some things that caused me to walk on the wild side and live a life not pleasing to God. I had been in a relationship after being molested and using drugs and alcohol. I continued drinking until I turned 20 when I got pregnant with my son. During this pregnancy, and just like I would be with my pregnancy with my little girl, I was on bed rest and had complications. My son was born premature and died a few hours later. To deal with his death, I began drinking and going out every night. Not sleeping or eating, I just wanted to die and be with my son. My relationship with his father, Todd, had ended. From my children's father, Todd, to my ex husband Scott, I felt like I always picked the wrong men. Not that they were bad men; just not the men for me. Instead of me waiting on God to lead me to the man He had for me, I was doing all the picking and choosing.

During this time before Scott, I was out of control. I was eventually taken to the hospital and put on a 72-hour hold. While there, I was given grief counseling. I was released under the condition of my attending AA. Although I didn't totally stop going out and drinking, I did slow down and would only do it on the weekends. Except for my relationship with Todd, my son's father, my life went back to normal after about 60 days. Todd and I still talked from time to time. I was close to his family, even attending church with them.

During the holidays, while hanging out with Todd and his family, I conceived another child. We got back together but it didn't last. After we broke up again, I later found out I was pregnant again and experienced another complicated pregnancy. When our daughter was born, she was in and out of the hospital with heart and pulmonary problems. The doctor said she would likely only live to the age of 3. It was extremely challenging. She went through years of surgeries and therapy, but she made it through. With God all things are possible! (Matthew 19:26) All you need is a mustard seed of faith. (Luke 17:6)

At my job, I met a group of people who were always happy and spoke about God as if He was their best friend and was always with them. I didn't understand. I was intrigued and wanted to know more. I started asking questions. I wanted to get to know Him better; to *"be in His presence"* as they would say. I learned about being saved and His salvation. I wanted to be saved. I became saved during a break at work. I began attending church and Bible study; even a single's Bible study on Friday nights. It was great! I loved the Lord and studying about Him.

Unfortunately, I allowed the enemy to step in and pull me out of the will of God. I became lonely during this time. This is when Scott came into my life. I started eyeing him at work and he is now my ex husband. I knew he was not the man God had for me. I thought I would just get to know him, maybe talk on the phone and just hang out from time to time. I didn't have a lot of time on my hands since I had a sick child who was in and out of the hospital. My daughter was getting therapy treatments twice a week; the other days I was in church. I just wanted someone to fill the little down time I had.

Before I knew it, I was in too deep. We were involved in sexual sin and the soul-tie had formed. I had one foot in, one foot out. I wanted to serve God and make Him happy, but I also wanted to make this man happy. There was no way I could do both. So I thought we should get married; that way, I wouldn't be living in sin. We both knew we weren't right for each other; we foolishly believed that getting married was going to make everything better. At least I thought it would. It only made everything worse. He wasn't living for the Lord and I was; well, at least I was trying to. I didn't drink or smoke; he did. All we did was fight. I wanted to live my life according to the Bible; he didn't. Now I know what they mean by being unequally yoked.

Not long after I got married, my happiness disappeared; the depression began again. My church attendance faltered after I had my second daughter. I began using drugs, smoking weed, and taking pills again. I would do anything to stop the mental and physical pain. I went to bed high; I woke up ready to get high. Smoking became the thing I looked forward to, more so than even going to church. My habit of waking up praying and going to bed praying ceased. I couldn't remember the last time I had prayed. I had forgotten all about God, but He didn't forget about me: He was still blessing me and working things out for my good. (Romans 8:28)

After a few years of the same routine of waking up high, getting high and going to bed high was all I wanted to do. I couldn't function without being high. That's what I thought. I was tired because this was all I felt I had: smoking, drinking, partying, and a dead marriage. I needed to change my life. I would always say to whoever would listen, "One day I'm going to stop drinking, smoking, and partying with Y'all and dedicate my life to the Lord." No one thought it was possible; they just laughed at me. I had to change my life. It was spiraling downhill fast. If not for myself, I had to do it for my kids. They deserved better.

I heard that song playing, "Wanna Be Happy?" 'YES!!' I said to myself. But where would I start?

I talked to Scott, my husband at the time, and tried to get him on board. He wasn't having it. He was neither trying to stop smoking and drinking nor trying to go to church. I had to do it all on my own. The kids and I started getting up on Sunday and going to church. Then I started praying. I began listening to gospel music. I didn't change overnight, but it was a start. It took time. It was hard. I had to eliminate everyone and everything I previously associated with: my friends, my family, even my husband. I stopped drinking first. Over time, I stopped smoking. Well, I would stop, but when something in my life went wrong, I would start all over again.

I'd found the answer before; I just had to remind myself that all things are possible through Christ that strengthens me. (Philippians 4:13) I sought Him and I found Him. (Deuteronomy 4:29)

I learned to replace the smoking with prayer. When something went wrong, I prayed. I've now been sober and clean for 5 years. Being in God's presence is better than any drug or sex that man or woman could ever provide. I am the happiest now than I've ever been. I give God all the glory. I couldn't have done it without You. Thank You.

Sharese Hudley

 Sharese is a single mother of two beautiful daughters, one adult with autism and an athletic teenager. She volunteers at her church and enjoys spending time with family and friends and doing outdoor activities. She loves cars and visiting the racetrack. Her dream is to one day work with kids with special needs.

✉ sharese.hudley@hotmail.com

Trust the Tug
Lori Ashworth

I remember so clearly the day GOD met me in one of the most important times of my life. My youngest son had recently been diagnosed with autism. I was one of those moms that had been going to Bible studies at our church for almost six years. Now, though, I was home with my son, trying to figure things out. It was just easier at the time to be home. So, I decided to have a few friends over and have our Bible study in our home!!

We were about three weeks into one of our studies and the words I had heard many, many times before spoke to me loud and clear: GOD IS IN CONTROL! Let go and let GOD!!

This journey of trying to figure our children out can get very tiresome. You can feel very defeated when you are faced with road block after road block.

From that day on I started to change my mindset and began to remind myself: in all things — GOD IS IN CONTROL!!!!

I started looking at things through a different lens because of this journey I never expected to be on; the journey no one ever expects to be on. I needed HIM. I needed big faith and trust!!!

When you are a mom {parent,} all you want is the best for your children, right? I had a nonverbal child until he was about 5 ½ years old. I remember the normal response when he was three: "Oh, he will talk. He has three older siblings doing all the talking for him." At three, that was somewhat reasonable, or at least I told myself it was; still a little in denial I am guessing. Then, when the diagnosis came and the scale of "Normal" markers was so off, it was clear to me just how behind he was. It was sad, so sad, to read that report and wonder if he would ever catch up.

My Bible study at our home started when he was about five. He would have been going into kindergarten after two successful years in preschool, but that transition brought on so much stress for him. A few weeks after school started, he began resisting me every morning, biting his fingernails, super anxious, still nonverbal. All I hoped and prayed was that, if he could at least communicate what it was, if he could tell me, I could possibly help him.

I decided to keep him home. Yes, with that came guilt. "If you don't push him thru school he will never learn anything; never have any friends. He needs structure. He needs therapy." And the big one, "What will people think?"

Letting go and letting God reminded me that God had a perfect plan for my son. It reminded me that God's plan for my son looked different than for other children. It also reminded me that if the typical plan caused him and I stress and anxiety, then maybe, just maybe, that wasn't the perfect plan for us.

During this time of discovery, I also remember people saying how sometimes kindergarten is a really hard transition for kiddos; yes, I had three kiddos before him that all went to kindergarten. It was different, and I wasn't just being an overprotective parent. I was learning to be ok with not doing what is typical, learning that each child is different, and this child was going to learn and grow differently - socially and educationally.

Let me back up just a little. A few years before my son came home from kindergarten, my oldest daughter had asked to be homeschooled. WHAT?? I was not equipped to home school. I knew a lot of mommas out there doing it in the community we had just moved to, but not ME!! I didn't have the patience. I had too many other things I wanted to do! I was actually growing a business at the time and knew that would change the looks of that for me.

Then, the year before my son came home, I realized that for whatever reason my daughter wanted to come home as a 5th grader, and now again going into

6th grade, I would figure it out. Whatever reason it was {life as a middle schooler isn't easy,} I wanted her to enjoy these years. Little did I know, she {GOD} was preparing me to have an open mind for keeping my youngest home a year later.

You never know why, you just have to trust God in this journey. Take a step, then, let go and let GOD. I call it TRUST THE TUG!!

This way of thinking has allowed me to realize that God has a plan for my child with special needs just as he does for my children that don't have special needs. If I try to control His plan, I miss out on so much freedom for myself and even freedom to be a mom for my other children. This experience has shown me that we all don't fit into the same mold for education and learning. We all don't need the same things to be successful. We do need the desire to be led by God to find our passions and use the gifts God has given us to live a long, happy, and full life.

I continue to be reminded of when God met me throughout this journey. I look back and think about who I was when my son was diagnosed and who I am now. God has taught me patience like no other; compassion for women and moms with children with special needs; compassion for the families living with children with special needs. He has taught me to be brave and have courage to take what I have learned and be there for others. He has further taught me that I need to embrace this journey and continue to rely on Him in all things.

God has allowed me to watch as my older children and husband learned to connect with our youngest in different ways. Many times it is easy to feel guilt that your children and family are missing out, but getting to the point of understanding how God allowed this child and these circumstances in our family so that somehow, someway we could all be used by this experience makes the journey look a little brighter. For His glory.

Lori Ashworth

Lori is a wife and a mother of four amazing children, her youngest happens to be living with autism. She has always had a passion for helping women which led her to start a non-profit called *The Circle Room*. Lori desires to build a community for families with special needs children which would provide activities, support groups, resources, respite and most of all grace, acceptance, and prayer!

✉ thecircleroomministry@gmail.com

f @TheCircleRoom

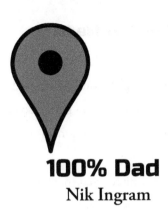

100% Dad
Nik Ingram

Hey! My name's Nik Ingram. I'm 35 years old and a husband, dad, follower of Jesus, entrepreneur, author…and a *forgiven* failure.

Of the 35 years I have been on this earth, it has only been in the last few months that I have realized that there has always been this one thing that has held me back in my life. I never really could put my finger on it. My wife would try to tell me what it was; my mentors would try to tell me what it was. But when I heard it out loud, I just could not believe that it was that simple.

When I was six years old, my biological father abandoned my sister and me. It's not the kind of story you might think of; you know, like he left us on the doorstep of an orphanage or anything. He cheated on my mom causing a bad divorce. It's not that he's a bad person, per se. In my mind, he has always been a good, outstanding person in the community and a successful businessman. I don't want to paint him in a bad way, but he is a lousy dad. And growing up, I never held that against him. I don't hold that against him today.

So, my mom remarried and my stepdad took the place of a father figure in my life. He taught me a work ethic and my mother made up for my dad's absence in huge ways.

Growing up, I didn't really fit in with the popular kids; my sister did. She was a cheerleader, then on the dance team, and very pretty. I, on the other hand, was just an average ordinary kid. I was pretty smart and I enjoyed school and learning.

Those who know me are not surprised to know that I wasn't involved in athletics. What I did love, though, was racing. Before I graduated from High School, my brother and I started racing go-carts. We had gotten so good that we were going to have to start traveling a lot. But something held me back. I was faced with a choice that would alter my life forever.

After I started racing go-carts, I discovered that we needed decals for the carts. So my stepdad actually said, "Hey, why don't you buy one of those machines that cuts vinyl and you can put decals on your go-carts and other people will probably want decals? Then you can make signs and all that stuff!" I thought that was a pretty cool idea.

At the time, I wanted to be an electrical engineer and was planning on going to LSU to get my degree. I had a plan. This decision to start this sign business completely disrupted my life...in a good way.

So I started with a cutter and a machine in my mom's living room. I'll never forget it. They helped me get a loan for $2,500 to get the machine to start making all the vinyl. My Mom and Step-Dad purchased my first few rolls of vinyl. Then, I sold it back to them in the form of decals and signs. What an entrepreneurial spirit, right? My mother pays for the materials and then I do the work and sell it back to her.

My friend and I remodeled a building we had on my parent's property to live in. I eventually turned it into my sign shop; I was pretty resourceful. I remember one day we needed a table. The only thing we could find was an old eighties model coke machine. I turned it on its back and I made my signs on top of it.

As I built my business, I had many downs and ups in my personal life: a broken engagement and some other relationships that didn't pan out. While serving as a youth pastor at my church, I met my wife. We were engaged two weeks later and married 4 months after that.

Fast-forward to December 2014: two days before Christmas, a tornado hit our town. At this time, Maggie and I weren't as involved in ministry: we were unsure of our purpose and mission. When the tornado hit, Maggie and I volunteered to help the town recover as a volunteer coordinator and case manager to help people who had lost their homes.

In those moments of devastation after a disaster, we realized that people were so vulnerable, they were looking for hope. We discovered that this was the most pivotal time to present Jesus to them. Many of those same people to whom we ministered are serving and loving God today. Many of the relationships I built in my life with the volunteers have developed into life-long friendships. I look back and realize that I didn't know anything about disaster relief. And now, I would have never wanted to live life without that experience.

That experience sent Maggie and me into this wild journey of understanding and acknowledging that this was our mission, our passion. This was a way for us to view and portray Christianity in its purest form. It was the most incredible ministry opportunity for us.

After we wrapped up the relief efforts, Maggie and I began the remodel of our own home. We faced so many things that most people our age didn't have to face. We were on a difficult journey. I came out of it extremely hurt and damaged. I became a recluse and dove headfirst into my business. It felt like that was the only thing I could have control over. I became an expert in marketing, sales, signs, and the digital aspects of marketing. I did it with such a different mindset and a different attitude.

I fell into a deep depression and a very dark time in my life. It was silent depression that no one really knew about. I felt purposeless. I felt like I could really relate to Moses. (Exodus 2) He ran out of Egypt after killing a soldier for his people and everyone was mad at him for it. He runs away and becomes a shepherd. I could see how during that time he probably felt depressed.

I remember praying a prayer when I first came to Woodlawn…"God, if all I do for the Kingdom is clean toilets, I'll be happy."

WRONG!

About 2 years later, Maggie got hired to work as the manager at our church coffee shop. I soon became the proclaimed dishwasher for a year and nine months! All I did was wash dishes while Maggie ran the coffee shop. I'm not going to lie;

at first, I did it very begrudgingly. At that time, that was literally the only thing I was going to church for.

I finally got to the point where I said, "Ok, I'm gonna come and be happy and I'll try to give this my best, even though I'm just a Dishwasher."

One day a friend and mentor of mine came into my office. He often counsels me when I have issues. He said, "Nik, you have a control problem. You suffer because of this abandonment from your father. And you just really haven't dealt with that."

I'm thinking, "But I don't even care." Like, "It's okay. My dad abandoned me. Who cares? I'm not going to cry about it. I'm not gonna whine about it."

He said, "Well, what this has done is caused you to keep yourself busy and keep yourself buried in your business and all the things that you think you need to do to give you peace and happiness. And the reality is this: God can't work through you and speak to you because you have these blocks and you don't trust God as your Dad."

We'd spent 8 years gradually moving away from what I'd felt was our purpose, while watching glimpses of opportunities seemingly disappear as quickly as they had arrived, and just like THAT...we were brought back to it.

It was like this: You know those old style sprinklers that turn in one direction, click-click-click-click-click, then go back the other way in one smooth, whoosh-move?

It was similar to the 40-year journey of the Children of Israel: it could have taken only 11 days. It took me a LONG time to get in position to hear God's specific calling and direction. Quite frankly, I thought it would take another 8 years to get our feet back on His divine path. It only took four days!

The Lord directed me to some Scriptures:
- The first was Romans 5:3-5 (KJV)
  And not only so, but we glory in tribulations also: knowing that tribulation worketh patience; And patience, experience; and experience, hope: And hope maketh not ashamed; because the love of God is shed abroad in our hearts by the Holy Ghost which is given unto us.

- Next was Hebrews 11:1 (KJV)
  Now faith is the substance of things hoped for, the evidence of things not seen.

This is how powerful this is…

- **Tribulation.** The junk of life; the ramifications of living in a fallen world. Tribulation brings patience…

- **Patience.** From patience, comes experience…

- **Experience.** In other words, you gain experience through the development and cultivation of patience. Experience brings forth hope…

- **Hope.** From experience, you gain hope. Faith is a substance; the literal holding of hope.

But faith is **not** the final step. For years I've lived by and taught the revelation that came from the preceding scriptures. Only recently have I allowed God to reveal that there's more to the process. Faith has to bring us to a place of love. The Lord showed me the clear path from faith to love through additional Scripture.

- 2 Peter 1:5-7 (KJV)
  And beside this, giving all diligence, add to your faith virtue;
  and to virtue knowledge;
  And to knowledge temperance; and to temperance patience;
  and to patience godliness;
  And to godliness brotherly kindness; and to brotherly kindness charity.

]Without tribulation, there is no faith. Without faith, there is no love. For it is impossible to please God without Faith. But it doesn't mean that God is pleased just because we have faith. We have to **ADD** to our faith…LOVE! And we can get stuck at the faith step, never reaching that place of having love.

The Lord revealed to me that I'd gotten to the faith step, but had stopped there to avoid pain. I kept myself busy. Every time someone hurt me, I buried the pain in the busy-ness of life. I kept learning more about marketing and creating businesses. I hired new employees to deal with "people" in my business so I could separate myself and recluse.

And that took me further into a downward spiral of disconnection from my authentic purpose. It also eventually caused me to live an unfulfilled life.

How?

I was a Bible-believing, Holy Ghost-filled, saved Christian, who had remained in control of his life. In fact, it can be said that I'm a bit of a control freak. I didn't believe it, though. This is what my wife and mentor had been trying to tell me. I considered myself the most flexible, understanding person I know. I guess I was just pretending I was that person.

Yes, I knew that God was God. It was easy to see Him as my Master, and I had no issues believing Him.

"God, I'm Your servant, everything is Yours, and I'll go where You want me to go. Direct my path."

I also had this mindset of, "I count on ME." I was determined to be in control because I knew that *I* was NEVER going to hurt me. If something bad happened, it was my duty to fix it. I knew I had the work ethic and the sense to work through any issue that came my way.

I counted on God to bless my ability and my strength. Although I loved Him and had trust for Him, it was still about ME and my abilities.

On one hand, there's 100% total control. On the other hand, there's the opposite: 100% complete dependence. I had to learn to navigate the journey between releasing total control and abandoning complete dependence to meet in the middle: 100% FAITH in the fact that I needed God to be 100% DAD in my life.

I never believed this affected me. Unfortunately, deep down inside I was hurting. I wouldn't and didn't want to believe that it was because of my relationship, or lack thereof, with my biological dad. I mean, so what I didn't have my dad? But so is the case with countless others. I wasn't going to cry about it. That wasn't going to get me anywhere.

Those abandonment issues prevented me from true and open fellowship with God because I needed to control everything; I couldn't surrender and rest in the arms of God the Father, who is 100% Dad.

My friend and mentor told me that because of my abandonment issues with my dad, I was experiencing trouble with and even blocked God from being who He wants to be for me: my 100% Dad!

Throughout this journey there have been "Father Figures" who picked up the slack in my life. There were also others who caused more pain, in turn, causing me to trust less and less. All of these men were and are gifts from God and have been instrumental in helping to shape who I am as a man.

For God so loved the world that He *Gave*...so that we could be transformed into His image. And that image is to be the Son of God.

God created Adam to be His first Son. When Adam failed, God had to send His second Son. Born of a woman, 100% man, 100% God, Jesus, the Son of God, sacrificed Himself for us. Love Brought Jesus to the cross; FORGIVENESS is the journey by which He got there.

In order to become the sons of God and allow Him to become our 100% Dad, we have to understand 100% forgiveness...for **that** is our ultimate purpose.

Nik Ingram

 www.LookAtGod.co

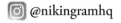 @nikingramhq

@nikingramhq

In Good Times and in Bad

Beatrice Bruno, The Drill Sergeant of Life

"Daughter, I am going to take your husband."

"The devil is a liar," I replied to this Voice.

"It is not the devil; it is Me," the Voice replied.

Amos 3:7 KJV *Surely the Lord God will do nothing, but He revealeth His secret unto His servants the prophets.*

Deuteronomy 18:22 KJV *When a prophet speaketh in the name of the Lord, if the thing follow not, nor come to pass, that is the thing which the Lord hath not spoken, but the prophet hath spoken it presumptuously: thou shalt not be afraid of him.*

These were words I neither wanted nor needed to hear at any given time in my life, especially concerning the love of my life on the earth!

Now, of course, you are probably a bit skeptical about the veracity of my above conversation with the Lord. Trust me; so was I. Why on earth and in Heaven's name would He first of all tell this to me? And then, why would He want to take my husband, someone He had allowed me to be with for so long?

The day God called my husband, Sergeant First Class (US Army Retired) John Patrick Bruno, Senior, home to Himself began like any other day. It was Tuesday, August 7, 2018. On Tuesdays, part of my usual routine was to go to the radio station to be a co-Host on The Good News with Angie Austin. I looked forward to meeting Angie and our other friends and producer Dave to talk about the

Good News. I didn't realize that by the end of the day, I would not have any good news.

As I prepared to leave the house that morning around 9:30 am, my husband and I bantered back and forth as per our normal routine. We laughed back and forth as I joked with him and him with me about this day.

I left the house at about 0945, my usual. I had fixed him breakfast and his usual coffee before I left. I stood at the front door, keys in hand and bag on shoulder, ready to go out the door.

"Sure do love you, Man!" I said across the living room to the family room where he sat playing his old Warcraft game on the computer.

"Sure do love you, Wo-Man!" he returned as I closed and locked the screen door, leaving the wooden door open to catch the intermittent breezes that morning.

I went out to our old truck that I had inherited when he purchased his coveted new 2017 Nissan Titan. He loved that truck! I was good with the 2007 model to get me to the places I needed to go.

I ran back in the house to his voice, *"What'd you forget?"*

He knew me so well. I always forgot something before I could get on the road.

That day was the usual: radio station, maybe a trip to the grocery store, maybe a trip to one of my bestie's houses after the radio station. It was one of those days that I wouldn't see him before he left for work. I wonder if I had known it would be that day that the Lord would call my husband home to Himself, would I have changed my plans to stay with him for just a few more minutes. I guess I will never know. **God met me here…**

I did not think back to the conversation I had had with the Lord approximately three years before this day. Nor did I flash back to the times He had briefly brought His words and promise to my mind since that original conversation. But, God did what He said… He met me there…

Now, knowing that no man knows the time nor the season when God will call any of us home, some might think I was fortunate that God would reveal such a thing to me. I don't see it that way. I didn't want to have to think of how my life would be without my husband. I didn't want to think about how our children -

Tara, William, John Jr., and EJ, and niece Jakeia - would feel at the loss of their Dad and Uncle. I didn't want to think about any of this stuff. But, **God met me here...**

Nevertheless, not my will but Thy will be done...

We exchanged several emails before the fateful call.

"Gas 47.00. I love you much." Him

"I love you much more. Have an awesome day." Me

"Gonna try, Beloved." Him

"Going to make a $200.00 payment to Capital One at lunch time. I love you." Him

"OK. Thanks." Me

I never knew that this would be the last conversation we would have. **God met me here...**

On August 7, 2018, at about 7 pm, God met me in the trauma room of University Hospital in Aurora, Colorado. I had received a call around 6:15 that evening from my husband's phone. When I answered the call on my cell phone, a woman's voice said to me, *"Beatrice, this is Claudia..."*

Now, not really thinking about something happening to my husband, I went the Southern route and thought to myself, "This had better be really good for some heifer to be calling me on my husband's phone." Seriously, that's what I thought. But, the next words took the very breath from my lungs...

"Beatrice, this is Claudia. John has collapsed and is barely breathing."

I had just left the Walmart Neighborhood Market near our home in Aurora. I had fresh chicken in the bags on the floorboard in the back seat of the truck. This was not happening.

I am going to take your husband...

All I could do was shake my index finger on my right hand at the window as I drove

"No, Lord! No, no, no, no! Not like this, Father!"

I was frantic and did not know what to do. I had the presence of mind to stop by the house to take the food I had just purchased to my mother-in-law and tell her I was on my way to the hospital to see about her son.

What? Not my husband, Lord!

God met me here…

How do you respond to something like this? He was with me the entire time as I listened to what Claudia was saying as I tried to think on what I was about to do. Those words are with me until this day, haunting me, causing me to rethink my position on life and living. I miss my husband. God did exactly what He said He would do. He met me…in a way I did not want to be met.

What do you do when something like this occurs in your life? Where do you turn to but the Lord? There is no one else…Only God can meet you in such a situation as this. And He did just that…

My beloved husband and I had such a wonderful life together. Although we never had enough money, never was able to take the time off for vacations and such, we had each other. I have learned that that is enough. It is all we really needed.

As I look back over my life, I realize now that God has been meeting me in life situations and circumstances all of my life. He has met me in ways I never imagined; I just never realized it.

I guess you wonder why I talk so much about God meeting me there in all of life. Well, I recognize that God has been with me through thick and thin. There has not been a moment in which He has not been with me. His word in Hebrews 13:5 comforts me that He will never leave me nor forsake me. I choose to believe Him. I take Him at His Word.

You see, when I was in High School and going through some things I should not have been going through, I did not know that, even in my sin, God was with me and would never leave me. Now, He didn't necessarily get my attention during this time. I knew a little about Him, but I was not a follower as I am today.

There were so many things going on in my life when I was a teenager. My grandfather, Freeman Stalworth, passed when I was 13. When he left the earth, his death took everything out of me. I didn't know what to do with myself. And I did many wrong things. Now that I look back over my life, I recognize that God met me right there.

Some friends once took me to a church, a Holy Ghost church. The preacher that night got right in my face. He spoke words over me. I remember him telling me that I was blessed. I didn't know what being blessed meant. I knew that my family and I had not been blessed up until that point. Not that I knew of. God was meeting me there.

God was showing me that there was hope for me. I had given up over the course of my life. When I became pregnant at the age of 16 and my family gave up on me, I gave up on myself. Even then, God met me there. He wanted me to know that there was still hope for me. He wanted me to know that I did not need to give up. I needed to keep moving forward so I could fulfill His will and purpose for my life. **God met me...**

He met me in ways I did not recognize because I had not received Jesus Christ as my personal Saviour. God never gave up on me. He never let me go even when I had reached levels of depravity that should have taken me out of this life. He wanted to save me. He wanted to make me over into something He wanted me to be. God *wanted* me.

On May 15, 1991, at the age of 32, I received Jesus Christ as my personal Saviour. It was the turning point in my life. When I said the sinner's pray that evening, I lay on the floor in a prostate position. I cried like a baby. Everything I had ever lived, every sin, came out of me that night. And **God met me...**

Do you want God to meet you? Just say this simple prayer...

Dear Heavenly Father, I come to you now, a sinner. Please forgive me for all my sins. I repent. Lord Jesus, come into my heart and be the Lord of my life.

Thank You, Lord, for saving me. In the name of Jesus I pray...Amen.

Now, watch God meet you...

Beatrice Bruno, The Drill Sergeant of Life

Beatrice is an Army veteran and former (but always and forever) Drill Sergeant. An ordained gospel minister and life and writing coach, Beatrice loves showing folks how to get over themselves and let go of the PAST.

And now, Beatrice has crossed over into an area few, if any, look forward to – Widowhood. Married for 27+ years to John who passed away in August of 2018, Beatrice has raised four children - his, hers, and theirs - to adulthood. Beatrice is now looking for her new normal…if there is such a thing…after losing her beloved husband. Now discovering what grief is all about and what it entails, Beatrice lets her audiences know that "you don't have to traverse the path of grief by yourself."

The founder and leader of POWWOW (Prophetic, On-Watch Women of Worship/War) Prayer and Conferences, Beatrice conducts Christian Women's Conferences around the world and also mentors youth.

In this season, God has called Beatrice to an RV Ministry: *The Drill Sergeant of Life Sermon-ator Mobile.* She will travel the country to where God desires and ministering in style God has given her for such a time as this.

Beatrice Bruno, The Drill Sergeant of Life, leaves no soldiers behind…no matter what branch!

 www.drillsergeantoflife.com

 @DrillSergeantofLife

It's Never Too Late
Donna Schooler

As a teenager growing up in the close-knit, family-oriented town of Pratt, Kansas, I spent every summer with my Grandmother Jesse, my Grandfather Henry, and my partner-in-crime cousin Tanya. I'm sure my mother Bette thought she was doing what was best for a teen with too much time on her hands during the Summer months.

My cousin and I were typical teenagers who, being required to attend regular church service whenever we could, would sit in the back of the church on those hard, wooden pews and mock the Pastor. It was hilarious. We knew the expectations; being young, we weren't ready to accept them. We spent what seemed like a month of Sundays at church. My Grandmother enlisted those old Church Mothers to sit by me, watch me, and ensure that I was behaving like the proper church girl I was raised to be. At the time, it felt extreme and restrictive. I do fondly recall one of the members, Miss Katie. She was also one of my Junior High School teachers. She was compassionate and patient, helped me with homework, and took a real interest in me. In hindsight, I know she gave me the best of her so I could be my best self.

But I just wanted to have some fun. I wanted to hang out with my friends and do more than just go to church. Don't misunderstand me: I very much enjoyed the times when we had family gatherings with good food, laughter and strong bonding time. However, as I grew into a young adult, I wanted to dabble in the world I felt I'd been denied. Part of me wanted to heed the teaching of my Mother and Grandmother; the sheltered church girl wanted to experience what I thought was 'real life'. I began clubbing, drinking, and smoking cigarettes. I was so naïve and hard-headed. I thought I knew it all!

I stopped attending regular church services, only showing up on Easter. I had become a backslider. All those years in the church had taught me about God, but I never developed a real, intimate relationship with Him. Exodus 20:12 haunted me, *"Honor thy Mother and thy Father that your days may be long upon the land...."* (NKJV) I wasn't ready to give up my new lifestyle.

I began dating a young man named Robert. He was so handsome with his smooth brown skin, sculpted body, and steel-gray eyes that could make your knees turn to jelly and your heart skip a beat. Oh, I just knew I was in love! I gave myself to him: mind, body, and soul. Several months into our relationship, I found myself pregnant. This was not an era in which pregnant, unwed young ladies were well accepted. I remember my mother being so disappointed. What was I to do?

Abortion and adoption were not as prevalent then as they are today, and they weren't an option I even wanted to consider. Ultimately, Robert, not wanting to get married, abandoned me. I knew I couldn't take care of a child on my own. I ended up marrying James who was willing to accept my daughter, Alicia, as his own. He was a military man. Not long after our marriage, I was plucked out of Kansas ("Toto, we're not in Kansas anymore!") and living in the urban hub of Berkeley, California.

It was a whole new world for me. The rolling fields of Kansas, now long gone, were replaced with bustling highways, fancy bridges, and tall buildings. I was most definitely out of my element. If I thought what I'd done in Kansas was rebellious, I was mistaken. I was treading on the devil's playground now.

I had become disconnected from God and from His Word. I foolishly neglected to spend time with Him. My plans to "get right" with Him and learn how to be the wife and mother HE desired were overshadowed by my own misguided choices.

Ezekiel 18:30 tells us to, *"Repent and turn from all your transgressions, so that iniquity will not be your ruin."* (NKJV)

My spirit was willing, but my flesh was weak. (Matthew 26:41, NKJV) I was lacking in humility and meekness before the Lord. I didn't want to seek God's face. I was still in my flesh and didn't really want to change. In my ignorance, I believed I had time to change. Later, I'd forgotten that tomorrow is promised to no one.

As my sham of a marriage began to deteriorate, I slowly began to realize how much I missed church; missed being around other believers. I had married a man who refused to set foot in a church. The closest we were to having God in our home was the big, white Bible with the gold embossed pages sitting on the coffee table, opened to (of course) Psalms 23. I wasn't picking it up and reading it; somehow, though, just seeing that scripture as I went about my household responsibilities gave me hope and strength. I began to realize that this was not the life God had for me. I just knew He had so much better.

Determined to turn my life around, I divorced my husband and moved myself and my daughter to Denver, Colorado where my parents were residing. It wasn't easy. I had gone to college while in California and obtained my degree in Nursing, but was not yet licensed. I worked as a waitress while preparing to take my State Boards. Little by little, God reminded me that He was with me and that He would provide for me and my daughter. His Word reminded me that *He would never leave me or forsake me.* (Joshua 1:5, NKJV) I began regularly attending church with my parents. I felt my life turning around. Within a year, I had obtained my Nursing license and began working in a local hospital. I was soon able to provide a stable home for myself and my Alicia. God was showing Himself faithful; I was not.

Once again, I found myself hanging with the wrong crowd. And like *"a dog returning to his own vomit,"* I repeated my folly. (Proverbs 26:11, NKJV) Through an acquaintance, I met another man, Alan. He was seven years my junior. I didn't let that deter me; another tall, sexy man showing me interest. I don't know what made me marry him. Maybe it was simply because he asked. Maybe it was because I wanted to build a family. Maybe I was just lonely. For whatever reason, I married him.

Two years later, I had another child: a son. We named him Nate. He was a joyful baby and his chubby little cheeks begged for my kisses. My little family was complete. My rose-colored glasses were in full effect…until the first time he hit me. Like many abused women, I forgave him. And like many abusers, he repeated the pattern.

I began working double shifts and overtime. I worked so much in part, because he wouldn't hold down a job; but more so, to avoid the rock in the pit of my stomach and raging adrenaline I felt when I was around him. This went on for 5 years. I let him talk me into moving to his home state of Alabama.

"The cost of living is lower. We can have a better life," he said. Worn down by the abuse and a sense of helplessness, I agreed.

Moving from where I had the support of my family to where his family lived did not prove to be in my best interest. Suffice it to say that after more years of abuse and broken promises, I barely escaped with my life. My grown daughter, now with a child of her own, moved in with her fiancée. Threatened by my husband, I had to leave our son behind. I was a broken woman. But God reminds us that He'll give us *"beauty for ashes, the oil of joy for mourning, and the garment of praise for the spirit of heaviness…"* (Isaiah 61:3, NKJV) I had to believe that somehow, someway, it was all going to work out.

After leaving yet another husband, I returned to Colorado. Once again under my parent's roof, I worked hard to rebuild my life. I made more mistakes, stumbled and floundered, eventually landing on my feet with a good job in a prestigious hospital and a small place I could call home.

Encouraged by the grace and mercy God was showing me, I began to really seek Him with all my heart. An inward change began to take place. I no longer desired to defile myself with alcohol, clubbing, and not-so- good-for-me men. I prayed. I read my bible. I cried out to God for myself and my children.

In Matthew 6:8, we're reminded that our Father knows the things we have need of …"before You ask Him." In less than a year, my daughter, realizing she, too, had married a man who was not God's will for her life, came to live with me. I had my daughter and my grandson. I was so thankful! A little more than a year later, and much to my surprise, Alan relinquished my son to me!

Together again, and in need of much healing, the three of us began attending a sweet little church I hold in my heart to this day. Alicia and Nate flourished with me as we submitted to the call of God on our lives. In time, God's time, I became the Church Mother and an ordained Missionary; my daughter Alicia, an Evangelist; and my son Nate, a Prophet.

Through the storms of my life, God always had a perfect plan. He met me in my rebellion and carried me through to victory. It's never too late to return to the loving arms of The Father. His thoughts toward you are *"…thoughts of peace and not of evil, to give you a future and a hope."* (Jeremiah 29:11, NKJV)

Donna Schooler

Donna Schooler was born in Pratt, Kansas and grew up around her grandparents in a loving Christian home. As a young adult, she stepped away from God and her life took a large spiral downhill. She experienced the trials of alcoholism, isolation, and low self esteem. Through God's love she was able to begin to step out of that desperate place. Through the turn of events in her life she realized it is never to late for God to meet you...where ever you may be. She is active in her church and loves to spread encouragement and The Good News of the Gospel on her Facebook page.

She is the matriarch of her family, being the mother of two children, grandmother to six, great-grandmother to three.

@NeverToLate.Colorado

The Dream
Nik & Maggie Ingram

…But the dream began with a nightmare.

Nightmare scenarios in life occur because of sin. Sometimes that's just the result of living in a fallen world. More often than not, though, the sin comes about because we do something that either God has expressly prohibited (committing sin) or by our taking actions without consulting Him first; you know, trying to force a godly situation from something that God isn't in! My nightmare was a combination of the two.

Before I begin, please don't think that this is going to be a bashing session on someone I was once involved with. That's not the truth at all.

This is designed to show how God can turn ALL THINGS, including our sinful choices, around for our good, and for His glory. Like the Apostle Paul says in Romans 8:28...

…And we know that all things work together for good to them that love God, to them who are the called according to his purpose.

You see, I was dating this girl, and I was convinced she was the one. A more accurate statement would be that I wanted her to be the one. What contributed to this was that she and I had been sinning together. Because of the nature of that sin, we felt more closely bonded than we would have if we'd displayed better self-control.

We were engaged, but she had broken off the engagement. To say I was devastated doesn't quite express what was going on. I wanted to kill myself, and I was driving down the highway, crying and wanting to die. It seems dumb now, but I felt like I had zero to live for.

I ended up in the neighborhood of the church I was attending. I pulled into the lot, walked up to the front door, and was surprised to find the door unlocked. I walked to the main sanctuary, went down to the altar, and started praying.

"Hey God...it's me...Nik. The guy who wants to do something for you, but I don't know what it is."

I cried, prayed, and talked to God for 45 minutes, just pouring my heart out to Him. I felt Him speak to me and say, "I need you here."

I went from complete emptiness to complete purpose in an instant.

Now don't get me wrong: I was still sad. I still felt depressed because of the heartbreak. But at least I knew that Jesus was walking with me as well as leading and guiding my steps. So I begin the journey to getting over her and focusing on God. After more trials and heartbreak, He placed me on the path related to my calling - the call to ministry.

Beginning in August, 2004, I started a 4-month long ministry training that focused on non-pulpit ministry duties. I started making friends with the other 11 guys in the program. Now one of the things about this training program was that we could NOT have a girlfriend or even behave in a "relationship-type" of way with a young lady while in this program.

It would be awesome to say that I demonstrated this amazing self-control and that the fruit of the Spirit was alive and active in me (which He always was and is). The truth? I was super shy and about as smooth as 40-grit sandpaper...which made it easy to stay away from the ladies.

Every day I went to the chapel to pray. I got extremely close with the Lord during this time. I had dreams; I had visions. The Lord and I shared an extremely close fellowship. Many nights I would fall asleep in the arms of God. It was a beautiful time in my spiritual life, and I'm both humbled and thankful that the Lord invested His time with me.

While I was there at the Chapel, I found a pamphlet that contained affirmations regarding our future brides. As an Ephesians 5 husband should, I was praying and speaking the Word over her each day.

One day, I decided to ask God to show me who my wife was. This was exciting for me because I'd actually had my eye on a few of the ladies at Alexandria. I was hoping that God would reveal which one she was. Crazy, right?

I decided to go on a week long, water-only prayer and fast. God helped and carried me through the week. While it was a spiritually rich experience, the vision of my wife didn't come to me in a dream like I'd thought it would.

Now what DID happen during this week of prayer and fasting was an excited phone call from my Mom.

"Nik! I met your WIFE! I met the woman who you're probably going to marry. She's involved in ministry, she loves to sing, and she's involved in her youth group at church. She's perfect for you! I even got her email address for you."

"She sounds PERFECT, Mom. How old is she?"

"Nik, she's 16. She just came to take her Sweet 16 pictures."

In addition to owning the go-kart track, my Mom was a photographer. So taking Sweet 16 photos was something she regularly did.

But here's the issue — I was *21!*

"Are you serious, Mom? 16?! That's jailbait!"

She persisted, but I brushed it off with something like, "Thanks Mom. I definitely appreciate it, but...nah. The girl I'm interested in is my age...and legal!"

I hung up the phone, forgot that conversation, and continued with my prayer and fast.

The week came to an end without any vision or dream on my part. Two weeks go by, and, praise God, I had the dream. In a dream, you can see so much more than what you see in the physical.

I saw inside this woman's soul, I saw her personality, her character, her nature, her goodness. I also saw her physical appearance. I saw her face, her curly, short, reddish-brown hair, a beautiful shirt, a very long jean skirt with bronze studs. What stuck out most to me was her hand in front of her chest, holding something.

I couldn't figure out what it was and what it meant. What also struck me was that I'd NEVER seen this woman before.

I'm a visual person; if I see a face, I remember a face. Even if it reminds me of someone else, I remember faces.

For the next two years, I was diligently searching. I was drawn to the similar aspects that these women shared with my dream girl...but they didn't look like her. Believe me...I SEARCHED, but could never find her.

On Tuesday night, July 18, 2006, I headed to church to start praying—a melodramatic prayer, I might add.

"God, it must not be in it for me to get married at 23. God I'm just not gonna get married."

I mean, I thought all my friends were getting married. They were in serious relationships, some of them engaged. I kept praying and decided to give God control. Smart move, right?

"God, I'm done looking. I'm not gonna look for anyone else. I'm just gonna follow you. Maybe the dream I had two years ago was the result of too much pizza. I mean, I can't find that girl anywhere. I've searched. If she existed, I'd have found her by now in my circle."

My "Circle" was a group of young Christians who gathered together, ate pizza, and went to conferences (where I'd look for this girl)... basically young Christian folks doing life together.

I convinced myself that if I was going to find her, it was gonna be through my circle.

I was serving as the youth pastor. The Lord had really moved in our student ministry, taking us from a single teenager to over 30 students! The next evening, Wednesday, July 19th, I'm at church getting the sound system setup for Wednesday night youth service.

I was digging in a box for cables and connectors with the service on my mind. I couldn't find what I needed, so I went to the sound booth in the main sanctuary to continue my search.

As I was digging in their box of cables and connectors, one of the older-than-me ladies, Sister Patsy, came up behind me. In her country drawl, she said, "Brother Nik, there's a girl out here and I invited her to the youth service and she don't wanna go. Her name's Megan. And I tell you what, I bet if YOU invited her to church, she'd probably come." Then she kinda hit me on the shoulder as I was getting up and she said, "Never know...might be your wife."

WHOA. Stop. Don't talk like that!

You see, Sister Patsy had a reputation for prophesying. She was always speaking words of truth and prophecy in church. She was very connected to God. So when she said something, IT HAPPENED!

I rebuked her. "Don't say stuff like that, because it could come true! I don't know what God has for my life, and you don't either!"

She giggled a bit, just as sweet as she could be.

So I walked around the sound booth to meet this girl and her grandmother.

I walked up and said, "Megan, I'm Nik."

Now here's where our stories might differ. She remembers things differently and hates when I tell how I remember it (but I'm writing the story, so…)

The way *I* remember it, when she looked up at me and said her name, she had a bit of drool running down the side of her mouth. (That's the part she HATES... because there really was no drool. I just think it's funny...)

She looked up at me with these wide eyes and said, "Maggie."

After a bit of an awkward pause, I said, "Ohhhh-kay...Maggie. Well I'm the youth pastor here, and we're having youth service tonight. I'd like to invite you. Would you like to come?"

Without saying anything she looked up at me with those same wide eyes and simply nodded. At this point, I think, "This girl is a little special."

I still needed to get things set up, so I chatted with her as we walked back to the youth area. Once we were there, I handed her off to some of the girls in the youth worship team that had arrived early. "Hey girls, this is Maggie and she's new with us tonight. You girls chat it up, be friendly."

I went back to working on set up and called my buddy BB to see where he was.

"BB, you're late bro. You comin'?" I asked him.

He sighed a bit and said, "Man...Nik...I forgot my guitar."

WHAT?!

BB had one job at this point in time... to play guitar for youth service.

"You forgot your guitar?! What?! You had ONE job to do! That was to play music and sing during youth service, and you forgot your guitar?!" I roared.

So I walk over to Maggie and the girls who were preparing their instruments and getting ready for worship while waiting for BB.

"Hey Maggie, can you sing?" I asked, out of the blue.

She stared at me blankly and just said, "Sort of."

"Great!" I answered. "You girls teach her the songs, and she's gonna sing with y'all."

I'm not sure why we needed one more singer. I've replayed this moment in my head thousands of times, and it doesn't make sense. But that night, we needed one more singer.

Now by this time, she's said very little to me. I wasn't concerned, but I didn't think anything of it.

As the music began playing, I finally exhaled with relief. "Okay, service started. I can breathe. Thank You, Lord."

I look up to the stage and they're all up there, singing. I look at Maggie, and while she's singing, I notice that her hand is on her chest.

...and THE DREAM HAPPENS.

I realized that what she was holding to her chest was a microphone. In that moment, I KNEW she would be my wife.

I was like, "Okay God. Once I finally gave up searching, You sent her to me."

Exciting right?

After the service, I called my Mom, absolutely jazzed up.

"Mom! I met my wife tonight!"

"What?! Tell me about her!" she said.

So I described the whole situation to her, and she interrupted me, asking "Nik, does her grandmother live near the church?"

"Well, yeah, Mom. Her grandmother lives near the church which is why they were there tonight. She's interested in our church," I answered.

Mom went through a series of questions. After getting a series of 'yes' answers from me, she said, "Nik! That's the girl I tried to introduce to you TWO YEARS AGO! That's Maggie Burns."

This same girl is the one my Mom had told me I would marry while I was on my prayer and fasting week! This was the fulfillment of the cry of my heart, a Psalm 37:4-moment.

I'd been saying, "I wanna meet my wife." And God did it! He introduced me to my wife.

Just two weeks after we met, I asked Maggie to speak at our youth service. She got up and gave her testimony at our Wednesday night service.

After the service, we all went to dinner at the China Star buffet. Kevin and Ashley, a couple from Maggie's previous church joined us. They had driven down from Hattiesburg to hear Maggie speak and get some ideas on how to grow their youth group…or so I thought…

After dinner, they asked, "Can we talk with you and Maggie for a minute?"

The four of us were standing in a circle. They said, "God brought us here and moved on us to tell you guys that God has put the two of you together as a team."

They kept using the word "team", but I read between the lines. I KNEW she would be my wife, but I didn't know if SHE knew. We decided to start praying. You know; a good ol' prayer meeting in the parking lot!

As I'm praying, I feel God telling me, "Nik, grab her hand. And when you do, you're grabbing the hand of your wife."

Kevin stops in the middle of prayer and says, "I feel like God is telling someone to do something, and they're not doing it."

WHAT?! This is crazy, like a movie!

So I grab her hand and the Holy Spirit just FALLS on the parking lot. We all start praying. I'm thanking Jesus; Maggie is crying; Kevin and Ashley are praying in the Spirit. Just as soon as we finished praying, Kevin and Ashley left.

I looked over at Maggie and said, "So…hey…I like you a lot."

She said, "I like you a lot, too!"

I had Maggie take one of the girls from the youth group home, and I asked her to meet me at the church. On my way to the church, I called my Mom and asked, "Mom, are we racing on December 2, 2006?"

Why December 2nd? I don't know. It was just the date I'd seen as a good day for Maggie and me to get married.

My Mom confirmed that we weren't racing, and I dropped the bomb on her. "December 2nd is the day Maggie and I are getting married."

Of course, she was screaming with excitement and jumping around. But, I HADN'T TOLD MAGGIE YET!

Oops.

I got to the church first, opened the doors, and went into the sanctuary. She came in just a few minutes later and I was blown away. She was so beautiful. I mean, I simply don't have the words to fully express the blessing of that moment and how she took my breath away as she entered the building.

Even talking about it 13 years later still makes my heart race and my face light up. The Lord had done work in a way that only He could. Look at God!

I looked at her and said, "Maggie, how's December 2nd sound for a wedding?"

She burst into tears and said, "That's the day I've always wanted to get married!"

I immediately called a friend of mine to come to the church because it wasn't a smart move to be alone with a female — especially since she was my fiancée!

We stayed up until 4 am, talking with one another, and literally getting to know each other. We'd met just two weeks before and were planning our wedding in exactly four months. The four months from then until we said "I do" were some of the craziest months of my life.

But we got married! God had given me a dream, and that dream came true!

Line In the Sand

Tracy Fagan

The thief comes only to steal and kill and destroy.
I came that they may have life and have it abundantly.
John 10:10 ESV

For those who have been around the church at all, this is a pretty popular verse. I have a very real example of how Satan came to physically destroy me - but God came and saved me so I may have life, and have it abundantly.

Let me start by saying, the devil is patient. He will ever-so-slowly start leading you down a slippery slope; and before you know it, you are very far from where you want to be - and in a place you never thought you would ever be.

I need to say up-front: the relationship I was in was my idea, not God's. Even though I was not living for God when I met this man, God was VERY clear that I should not be with him. I have to say, my parents and friends were pretty clear in voicing that concern as well. However, I convinced myself of the following: "I know what I am doing. They are all wrong. They don't know him like I know him." Therefore, I didn't heed their warnings and stayed with him.

I will admit that we did have some good times. During our relationship, we started getting involved with many things that invited the enemy into our lives. Also, neither of us was saved, so our guiding morals and values were based on what **we felt** were ok. In tapping into our desires, feelings, and emotions, the enemy had a very easy time of luring us into the world of pornography and swinging. In my spirit, I will admit I knew it was wrong. However, in the moment, I wanted to please my partner and my own flesh. After each encounter was done, the letdown was big. I wanted to go take a shower because I felt so gross and dirty. The thoughts of, "Why am I not enough?" and, "Why would he want to share me?" began to tear down my self-esteem.

As much as I hated it, it was also feeding the lust that was in me. In the moment, it was making me feel wanted and loved (well, sort of); after the fact, each time, I felt lonelier. It was the result of using the precious gift God gave us for intimacy between a husband and wife outside of the confines of how it was intended to be used.

One of the slippery slopes that living the swinging lifestyle opened was the fact it began to blur the lines of what constitutes "cheating." Now, in the eyes of God, any physical/sexual actions outside of marriage are sin. However, when we began to make our own rules, we came into agreement that it was ok to sleep with other people. So what is the difference between us being with another couple together and him being with a woman without me? The rules were so wishy-washy. They were based on our feelings and shifting morals - not the truth and the Word of God.

"Everyone then who hears these words of mine and does them will be like a wise man who built his house on the rock. And the rain fell, and the floods came, and the winds blew and beat on that house, but it did not fall, because it had been founded on the rock. And everyone who hears these words of mine and does not do them will be like a foolish man who built his house on the sand. And the rain fell, and the floods came, and the winds blew and beat against that house, and it fell, and great was the fall of it."

Matthew 7:24-27 ESV

During this time, the enemy continued to eat away at my self esteem and self worth. I was worn down, empty, and broken. Then we came to the night that would be the beginning of the end of this nightmare. We had a party at our house;

we had all been drinking. Along with being depressed, my mind was clouded by alcohol. As the night was coming to an end and people were leaving, my man insisted on walking this woman to her car. I watched from our bedroom window as he escorted her to the car and began passionately kissing this woman goodnight outside our brand new house. I lost it. I was an emotional wreck. After he came back in, we briefly fought; he went to bed.

I had lost all hope. At that point certain details got very fuzzy while others became very clear. It was kind of an out-of-body experience. I went down to the kitchen and grabbed a knife and held it to my wrist. I remembered hearing someone say to hold it parallel to your arm, not perpendicular, so it is right along the vein. That way you would get a good cut and lose blood more quickly. I remember thinking, "I would NEVER think of committing suicide." However, by that point, I was so crushed, hurt, and hopeless - there I was. I do remember there being many voices in my head, condemning me for so many things - the lifestyle I had been living, the position I had gotten myself into, the fact I couldn't be enough or do enough to please my partner...the list went on.

Then, I heard a very strong, loving, caring, and clear voice that was above all of the other voices. "This isn't the answer. Your daughter needs you. Put the knife down." I remember obeying...immediately. I put the knife down. The taunting evil voices stopped.

I went upstairs looking for help and comfort from my man. Instead of support, I received belittlement and condemnation for my selfishness. I went downstairs and spent the rest of the night by myself. Although I was by myself, I remember not feeling alone. Among all of the chaos, there was that peace that surpasses all understanding (Philippians 4:7), and a clear path as to the next steps (Psalm 37:23.) I began to search for a counselor I would call the next day.

I didn't know it at the time, but since then, God has revealed to me that Satan's plan that night was to kill me, but God drew a line in the sand. I was spiritually so opened to the enemy and his evil ways, I had become tormented and trapped. But God! But God! But God! God came to me that night so that I may have life, and have it abundantly. God kept me.

Exactly one week to the day from that situation, my partner asked to end the relationship. I would have never left on my own. Once he said he wanted to end it, I felt an immediate strength come over me that kept me from going back.

Tracy Fagan

 Tracy Fagan is a fireball for Jesus and in life. She has experienced the transformational, healing love of Jesus in her life and loves to share that with others through books, speaking, and teaching.

She is the founder of *Kingdom Publishing*, a Christ-centered book publisher. She uses over 24 years of marketing experience, her creativity, and encouragement to help others fulfill their God-given assignments and bring their ideas and stories to life.

She loves her native state of Colorado as well as experiencing different cultures through travel. She loves to hike, ski, workout, dance, and most of all, laugh. She is a proud mother to a beautiful daughter.

🌐 www.Kingdom-Publishing.com

📘 @Kingdom.Publish

📷 @Kingdom.Publish

Temporal Sight
Teresa Blaes

There you were, always shifting
Guess I always thought that you would be there.
But I did not realize that you were slipping away,
Not 'til I awoke to discover it was too late.
I remember it like yesterday--
The day I went under the knife.
The Doc swore he'd do all he could
To restore my temporal sight.
But in that moment, time stood still.
With pokes and prods I learned heaven's will.
"Too much scarring," I heard him say.
And then a temporal cadaver remained--
Everything I thought once mattered;
My faith once strong, now shredded and shattered.
Years I traipsed through that desert waste.
Heaven was to blame!
I went to church when it was expected
Only to retreat, His message rejected.
Yet even still-- an ember remained ,
And if I listened I'd hear His whisper.
Slowly the ember brightened to a spark.
Death transformed to life inside my heart.
I still lack temporal vision--
But with ears wide open I've begun to listen.
Eternity is just a breath away,
And on that day, I will see the face
Of the One who bore the nails and took my place.

It started at 4 am.

I had gotten up to take care of something when Mike's phone rang. My dad was in hysterics on the other line. He had come home to find my mom dead on the living room floor. Little did I know that this would be the beginning of a five-year journey that would test my faith to the breaking point. Yet, this journey would also be the most important place where God would find me.

Before the pain pills destroyed her life, my mom was the coolest person I knew. She became addicted to opiates; and at one point, Mike and my dad were desperately trying to help her manage them with little to no success. They would lock them up in a safe and distribute the medications on schedule. My mom figured out a way to break into the safe. They finally gave up. To this day, I do not know if my mom died of an overdose or if she took her life deliberately by taking too many pills.

This, however, would not be the only testing of my faith.

The day after my mom died, I was scheduled for one last surgical effort to save what was left of my sight. Up to this point, I had hundreds of operations on each of my eyes. This included having my left eye removed due to it collapsing in on itself.

As it happened, I hit my head a few weeks earlier and went from being able to see as good as I have ever seen, to being completely blind in the span of a few hours. The doctor told me that the retina had detached and that we could try one last time to restore my sight.

Mike did not want me to go through with surgery considering I had just lost my mom. But if there was one thing I believed about my mom, I knew she would have wanted me to fight to restore my sight. I chose to go ahead with the surgery.

The day of the surgery came and they did all the pre-op activities. They wanted me to be awake during the actual procedure so I could tell them if I could see anything as they were working. I was put to sleep so they could numb my eye, then, awakened in the operating room.

Laying there, feeling all the manipulations of the tools, I heard them talking above me. To this day, I will never forget what was said... "There is too much scarring. I can't do anything."

In that moment, it all crashed around me. Everything I thought I believed was called into question. My mom was dead. My sight was as good as gone. My faith died right there on that metal operating table.

Was all this Christian stuff for nothing? Were all the years of trying to live as a believer in a non-Christian home a waste of time? I didn't have the answers just then, but I knew that I wanted nothing to do with God if He was so cruel.

As it turned out, I chose to have the eye removed. There was nothing more they could do to save it. Besides, I was in tremendous pain that completely debilitated me.

I believed that this was the final straw between me and God. All my life there was this battle between me and the glaucoma eye condition with which I was born. Each year, my eyesight grew worse. As a child, I endured surgery after surgery to fight it back. The choice to give up the eye felt like one last gut punch from God when I was already down.

Although I did not voice my unbelief, as the years dragged on, it came out in other ways. In an effort to escape the pain with which I was dealing, I became addicted to text-based gaming.

All the while, Child Protective Services and other related organizations were coming after Mike and me because they believed we were too blind to be parents of our special needs kiddo, Mandy.

I became very angry and depressed. But whenever I was asked if I was angry or depressed, I denied it. All that mattered for me was the gaming. I wanted nothing to do with the hell going on around me.

It was around this time that Mike called in our pastor to help. All they saw and understood was that I was addicted to the gaming. Neither Mike nor my pastor knew that I had walked away from God and was having a crisis of faith. This nearly destroyed my marriage.

All of this led to an event a few years later at a women's conference at Mike's parents' church. To this day, I remember very little about what the keynote speaker spoke on. What I do recall, though, was my encounter with her afterward.

She came to find me, walked up to me and placed her hand on my cheek, and said, "You are going to be a public speaker."

I didn't know what to make of that. However, all through the conference I could kind of hear the voice of the Father. In my mind, He was so distant– so far away.

For the previous four years, I had barely heard the voice of God. I believed in Him, but wanted nothing to do with Him. However, I knew that this was a Word directly from the Throne. I had no clue what to do with this Word; and honestly, so what? Why would He want anything to do with me? I thanked the speaker and filed that away in the back of my mind under lock and key.

A couple months later, I went to another conference with the women at my church. Even though I didn't want to go at all, Mike insisted. In fact, God apparently wanted me there because one of the ladies who had planned to attend ended up canceling. My ticket cost me nothing.

The conference was at a camp up in the mountains with no Internet connection. This meant no gaming; no place to hide. God had me right where He wanted me.

Mike kept telling me not to take my laptop because I would have no Internet connection. Did I listen to him? Nope.

Over the next three days, I listened to multiple speakers and participated in prayer sessions each day. It was during one of these sessions that I heard the voice of God more clearly than I had heard Him in a long time.

I had just answered a question, and He spoke to my spirit. "You're still angry at Me over your blindness."

I paused and answered Him, "Yeah, and...?" This was the first time in a long time I had had even a semblance of a real conversation. This was the beginning of a long journey back to Him.

My next encounter with Him at the camp was during one of the breaks. I was using the restroom and He spoke to me out of the blue. He asked me if I remembered some of the things that had happened to me as a kid. I answered yes. He asked me to write a book around those experiences. My answer was less than thrilled. In fact, it was outright refusal. Still, at least I was keeping the dialogue open.

On the last night of the camp, I had one final encounter. It was during an overflow worship service. The teaching had concluded and I felt His presence so strongly. I was talking to one of the ladies who had become a friend and began to open up about some of the pain I had been carrying from way back in my childhood.

I can truly and honestly say that it was in this moment that God met me. In this moment in the mountains, the King of all Kings met me. And He didn't chastise me for walking away or for the gaming which had become an idol to me. He just met me. Together, we began the journey to wholeness.

I will not say it has been easy, but it has been worth it. Out of my walk with Him has come a podcast, and yes, I am working on the book He asked me to write.

My hope and prayer is that my story will encourage you. God will meet you in your pain, no matter how deep that pain goes.

Teresa Blaes

Teresa Blaes is an author, poet, blogger, and podcaster. She is the founder of *Unresolved Life Ministries*, and is the host of the Unresolved Life podcast, a show seeking to answer some of life's most difficult questions. She is happily married to Michael Blaes and has an 11-year-old special needs daughter named Mandy.

www.Unresolved.life

@UnresolvedLife

@UnresolvedLife

A Place Where I Became Desperate

Dr. Jimmie Reed

There are times in our lives in which we encounter a situation where we realize it's beyond our ability to solve. Once we come to the conclusion that it is an impossible situation, we can experience feelings of desperation. In the summer of 1984, I had this experience.

While staying in a hotel in Geilenkirchen, Germany for eight weeks, my three-year old son became very ill. A severe asthmatic, he had contracted pneumonia. The military base we were assigned to did not have a hospital. It was recommended that I travel to Holland to the hospital because the Dutch culture had mastered the understanding and speaking of English. In fact, many of their television programs were in English.

My teenage daughter, my three-year old son, and I set out on the autobahn highway about 3:45 am to find the hospital. After traveling for over 40 minutes, we were not able to locate the Dutch hospital in the dark. Out of desperation, I began to pray in tongues. I found myself driving along what looked like a residential neighborhood. This neighborhood had a road that was divided by a strip of land with trees. One side was two lanes going in one direction; on the other side of the road, you could travel in the opposite direction.

As we traveled at a speed of only 25 miles an hour, about three-quarters of a mile down the road to my left, I suddenly noticed a small white vehicle with bright lights. It was stationary.

I didn't think much of it until I noticed it was positioned in the opening between the two sides of the road. Because my vehicle was the only other vehicle on the road, this other vehicle could have continued to move. It did not. By now, it was about 4:30 AM with no sign of daylight.

As I continued driving, the attention of my daughter and I shifted from looking for the hospital to focusing on the car that wasn't moving. All of a sudden, my heart began palpitating. I felt that something supernatural was about to take place, but did not really know what to expect.

Out of instinct, I turned my vehicle left, stopping directly in front of the little white car. I rolled down my window. In the other vehicle, a beautiful woman with the most intriguing, piercing blue eyes that seemed to penetrate right through me, looked up and said these words, "How may I help you?"

Because this one that appeared to me in human form seemed to be so much more, I said with much calmness, "My son is dying and I cannot find the hospital." I no longer felt desperate. Even though I did not know much about such things, I really believed this was some type of spiritual encounter.

She said, "Come and follow me." She did not ask me anything about the situation. She only spoke those words.

I followed her for less than a mile and was led to the guard gate of the emergency room entrance. I turned right to go towards the hospital. My daughter and I immediately looked back. There were no signs of any vehicle on the road; no car lights in the distance were evident. Looking at each other with amazement, we quickly returned our hearts and minds towards my son.

He lay on his back in my daughter's arms. You could see the bones in his chest protruding as he labored to breath. When the doctor's in the ER put the needle in my three-year old son's vein, he didn't flinch or move in any way.

Seven days later when my son was released from the hospital, the doctor told me they were not sure if they could save him. I learned later that one of the meanings of the number seven is 'completion.'

My story depicts how and where God met me, a desperate young woman with my 14 year old daughter on a dark road, lost in a foreign country with a very ill son and how He saved us all.

Dr. Jimmie Reed

Dr. Reed is the Senior Leader for *Global Manifestations*, in Pueblo, CO. Through practical application and demonstration she helps to prepare individuals for the work of the ministry.

Dr. Jimmie Reed combines dynamic teaching with compassion and wit while seeking to help bring Heaven's direction to the lives of individuals, to churches, and cities. Ordained through Springs Harvest Fellowship, by Apostle Dutch Sheets, Jimmie is recognized among ministry leaders as a prophet called to the body of Christ. In addition, Jimmie is ordained as a Christian International Prophet by Bishop Bill Hamon of Christian International Network of Churches.

De-mystifying prophetic ministry is a prime focus of her teaching. Called by God to equip believers, she imparts revelation from the Bible to help others become more acquainted with God's voice. "We are able to help each other enter into a deeper walk of intimacy and victory when we allow the Holy Spirit to minister His life through us," says Dr. Reed.

Dr. Reed has a schedule that incorporates leading seminars, conferences, retreats, church services, and prophetic classes where she equips, trains, and activates the saints in apostolic and prophetic ministry. Jimmie carries an anointing for 'BREAKTHROUGH' in many different areas of the lives of those whom she imparts and has begun to move out in signs, wonders, and miracles.

🌐 www.GlobalManifestations.org
📘 @GlobalManifestations

A Swim with the Angels
Linda R. Robin

I have been blessed with a wonderful, and in many ways, extravagant life. I know my Heavenly Father has been with me since He placed me in my mother's womb. I thank Him often for the family He gave me. My mother was no ordinary woman. She was caring, nurturing, beautiful, and kind; full of God's joy in all situations. My mother taught me about Jesus. But it was my own personal relationship with my Lord and Savior that was strengthened when He didn't just meet me…He kept me.

I was born in Bluefields, Nicaragua. I am number four of eight children given to a handsome couple. When I was a baby, my parents bought an old coffee plantation. It was located at the outskirts of the Masaya Volcano in the Ticuantepe region in the western area of the country. The setting was a utopia! There was lush vegetation and incredible flora and fauna. Our plantation was home to flocks of parrots, parakeets, toucans, and colorful singing birds. These wild, feathered friends serenaded us every morning.

On top of the adventurous landscape, the Mayan Indians once thrived in this region as well. As the coffee trees were planted, there was a treasure of pottery found from these ancient people. My home was the perfect playground for the adventurous tomboy I was!

It was interesting to discover that when my parents purchased the plantation, it was called Palestine. The previous owner was of Arab descent. Now for a quick history lesson, Palestine, now called Israel, is the small area of land in the Middle East that the Bible refers to as, "The Promise Land." It was the special land God promised to His children. (See Genesis 15:18-21) People have fought over this very fertile and sacred land for many centuries. Our family's plantation was like our very own Promise Land from God!

The process of farming coffee is magical. The luscious green trees bud with beautiful white flowers. As they open their petals, the rolling hills turn into a flowing lace blanket releasing a fragrance that makes your nose smile. The wind carries the unique, sweet scent for miles. The flowers expire and fall, leaving a small bean that becomes chameleon-like and gradually turns from bright green to gold to umber to persimmon to burgundy. The burgundy beans were a sign of joyful times!

The coffee pickers celebrated the important job of harvesting the beans through their jokes, singing, and laughter. Once the beans were picked and gathered, they were placed in a large cement pool, about 12 feet square and 6 feet deep, then stripped and washed of their sweet outer coating. All this was done in preparation for drying the beans in the warm Nicaraguan sun.

It was a typical, warm day in my life with the cooling currents of the fall air being felt. The coffee harvest was close which meant there was a bustle around the plantation. The washing pools were cleaned and being prepared for their part in the harvest process. The cool, clear water was calling me for a refreshing escape from the warm day. Even though we weren't supposed to swim in these pools, the 12-year-old tomboy in me was easily persuaded! I ran up to the main house, donned my bathing suit, grabbed a large towel, and headed to the tepid water that invited me to play!

I reached the edge of the pool with great excitement and anticipation. I leapt off the edge and dove straight down...my head found the bottom of the pool with all my weight and speed crashing into it. In a moment, tragedy attempted to interrupt paradise. I felt the blow on my neck and blacked out...

The next thing I remembered was a bright light covering me. I felt a strong grip on my arms and saw two glowing angels around me as they pulled me out of the pool and placed me on the side. Then I heard a loud voice in my head assuring me, "You are safe, My child."

God met me there right at the bottom of that pool!

We were raised Catholic. Until I developed my personal relationship with God through Jesus Christ, I did not fully understand that God has always been there for me....in all seasons.

The God I know sees and feels my every hurt and rejoices in every accomplishment! As long as I am humble and ask from the heart, He will continue to guide me. He will be there for you, too, if you just ask Him.

Linda R. Robin

Linda R. Robin and her late husband founded *The Healing Place for Veterans*, a non-profit organization that uses Arabian horses to offer therapy for individuals and their families who are impacted by PTSD, concussions, and special needs such as Autism.

"Life, after all, is what you strive to make it. With God all worthy causes are possible!"

✉ thehealingplaceforveterans@gmail.com

⬛ TheHealingPlaceForVeterans

📷 @HealingPlaceforVeterans

Wrap Up

After reading these stories, now the question becomes personal, "What do these stories have to do with me?" As you look back, I am sure there are one or two stories that resonate with you more than the others. Some might have been encouraging while others might have even made you feel "a certain kind of way" about how God let the story play out. You may even be upset that God is letting a similar story in your life play out differently. The reality is, God is an all knowing God and He does know what is best for you and me. Through these stories, you can see His character and His love for His children. Ultimately, He wants you to seek Him, love and trust Him, and most importantly, call Him your Heavenly Father.

For many of us, it can be hard to love God and trust Him because of the pain and trials we have experienced. You can see this truth pointed out in many of the stories in this book. God never intended for us to live that way. He wants you to be healed and made whole; but that requires you to want that healing, give Him your broken heart, AND allow Him to work in your life.

He has given us free will which means we have the opportunity to choose what we do, who we listen to, and where we put our priorities in life. If you choose God, He will come into your life and heal every broken spot you allow Him to touch. As you have heard in many of the stories, it is a process. However, it is a process that He will faithfully complete if you choose to start it and stick with it.

An important theme that ran through these stories is that the walk here on earth is not done alone. The authors mentioned others that came along side, including counselors, mothers, fathers, spouses, daughters, grandmothers, pastors, strangers, and friends. Many times God will send someone to speak to you, be with you, or even just pray for you.

The truth is, no one is ever the same after an encounter with God. Take notice how the course of each person's life took a new direction once God met them. It included surrendering to His will. It showed up in the stories as admitting an anger towards God, seeking counseling, leaving a toxic relationship, walking away from drugs and alcohol, trusting God, moving to a new city, giving up an addiction, or being ok doing things differently than the rest of the world. This step isn't always easy, but I promise you, when you choose to deepen your relationship with God, it will ALWAYS turn out good in the end!

So the question is, are you ready for God to meet you and radically change your life? He is reaching out to you right now and excited to move in miraculous ways in your life. The first step to a relationship with God is accepting the sacrifice that Jesus made for you and receiving your salvation through Jesus Christ.

Jesus said to him, "I am the way, the truth, and the life.
No one comes to the Father except through Me."
John 14:6 NKJV

Salvation: A Relationship with Jesus

You don't have to look very far to see that we live in a fallen world, one that is filled with pain, temptation, and sin. The Bible says we are all sinners and fall short of the Glory of God. (Romans 3:23) The payment for our sin is death. However, God's gift, if you choose to accept it, is eternal life in Christ Jesus. (Romans 6:23)

God so loved the world, specifically YOU, that He sent His only Son, Jesus. If you believe in your heart and confess with your mouth that you are a sinner and you need a Savior, and that Jesus came and died on the cross, was buried, and rose from the dead as payment for your sins, then you are saved! (John 3:16, Romans 10:9-10)

If you are ready to accept Jesus as your Lord and Savior, say this prayer out loud: Heavenly Father, I admit I am a sinner in need of a Savior. I believe that You sent Your Son Jesus Christ into this world as a sacrifice for my sins. I believe that He died, was buried, and on the 3rd day, He rose from the dead. I repent and turn from my sin and invite You into my heart. Jesus, I thank You for Your sacrifice and believe that You will protect me, guide me, and be with me. Amen.

Now that you have said that prayer and are saved, it is important that you become connected to the Body of Christ so you can learn more about who God is, study His Word, and receive the connection with other believers that is necessary. Ask God to lead you to a Bible-based Christian church in your area and get connected.

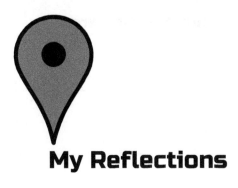

My Reflections

As was mentioned at the beginning of this book, it is no coincidence that you have this book in your hands. Each and every story was divinely authored, selected and written to touch someone who will read it. More importantly, I believe God is asking you to reflect back on times in your life where He met you. Even if you didn't know Him or believe, He was still there.

Take some quite time to reflect on your life. Ask God to show you where He met you along the way! Be bold enough to ask God the questions you hold deep in your heart. Journal your own story here.

_____

_____

_____

_____

_____

_____

_____

_____

A Bit About the Bible

You may have noticed that there are many references to the Bible throughout this book. If you have never really read the Bible, I would encourage you to grab one and read it! It is a fascinating book filled with intriguing stories of romance, betrayal, battles, victories, beheadings, and infidelity…but more importantly reconciliation, forgiveness, and love.

Some say the Bible is "Basic Instructions Before Leaving Earth." While reading and studying it, you will come to know who God is and how to live a victorious life. In the Bible, Paul explained it to his student Timothy in this way:

All Scripture is given by inspiration of God, and is profitable for doctrine, for reproof, for correction, for instruction in righteousness, that the man of God may be complete, thoroughly equipped for every good work.
2 Timothy 3:16-17 NKJV

You can find a physical copy of the Bible at any bookstore and even some big box stores. In starting out, I would recommend getting the New King James Version (NKJV) or the New International Version (NIV).

You can also download one of many Bible apps on your phone. This will allow you to flip between various translations. You can also sign up for different study plans and even receive a verse of the day.

When you start reading, don't let yourself get overwhelmed. This is a life-long relationship that God is calling you into!

Meeting With God

If God has met you in the pages of this book, we would love to hear about it. It is encouraging to hear how God has used our testimonies to touch the lives of others. It also gives us the opportunity to thank God and pray with you! Please visit our website or connect on social media and share with us.

🌐 www.Kingdom-Publishing.com
📘 @Kingdom.Publish
📷 @Kingdom.Publish

CPSIA information can be obtained
at www.ICGtesting.com
Printed in the USA
LVHW040155191219
641008LV00003B/44/P